Through The Bible In

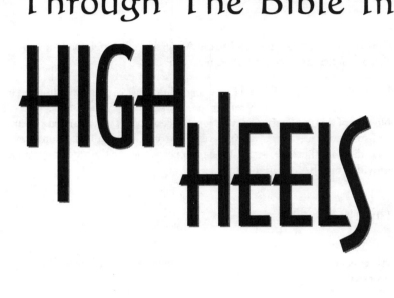

HIGH HEELS

Alice Hellstrom Anderson

Published by

Guardian BOOKS

Dedication

For Ivy

*Whose Spirit
Lifts My Own*

Table of Contents

Introduction

It is my firm belief that God has a healthy sense of humor, and it pops up throughout the Scriptures. Take Rahab, for example, the harlot from Jericho. Rahab literally means *broad* in the Hebrew language. I think it's just too coincidental that in today's vernacular, sometimes women of less than stellar morals are referred to as *broads*.

In my attempt to make the women of the Bible real and relevant to the lives of women today, I've taken a few leaps of imagination. Everyone knows that Eve didn't use Bisquick, of course, but her frustrations after she gave in to Satan's temptations were the same type that women experience today as we try to balance motherhood, housework, and making time for our husbands and ourselves. In Ecclesiastes 1:9 we read, "There is no new thing under the sun." Human nature is basically the same today as it was thousands of years ago.

Having said that, I want to assure you that in preparing these personal glimpses into the lives of the women of the Bible, my research is my own, and I have taken no theological liberties to make the stories read better. When it comes right down to it, I doubt that I could have invented some of the scenarios that God included in his Word. Whenever I exercised my creative writer's license to imagine what a certain situation must have been like, it will be very evident to the reader.

Women today need to know that God not only loves us, he understands us. As the wonderful song says, "No one understands like Jesus."[1] He cares about every last trivial detail of our everyday lives. He's not too busy to hear a woman's heart break because she cannot conceive a child. He's not too serious to chuckle when a woman meets the love of her life the one time she is covered with sweat and dust and wearing her oldest clothes. And he's not too far out of human reach to feel our hurts, our pain, and our longings to be loved for who we are. After all, our God became a human being so he could rescue us from everlasting separation from himself. In doing so, Jesus experienced every emotion we experience. How could he *not* understand what you are feeling right this minute as well?

This book was never intended to be all-inclusive; therefore, you won't find every single woman mentioned in the Bible within these pages. You may be tempted to read these chapters randomly, but please remember that this is a start-to-finish survey (or overview) of the Bible. It follows a historical thread, including the 400 years between the Old Testament and the New Testament. The history of the human race has continuity to it. It will make more sense to you if you read it in order the first time. You can always go back and read your favorite parts again. It is my prayer that you will grow closer to God by reading these insights he has given me to share with you, woman to woman.

Alice Hellstrom Anderson
Restoration Cottage
Maine

[1] *No One Understands Like Jesus*, John W. Peterson, © 1952, Norman J. Clayton, Melodies of Praise. International copyright secured, assigned to Norman Clayton Publishing Company.

Eve

Going Where No Woman Had Ever Gone Before

Personally, I have always felt Eve gets a bad rap from most people. She was the first person to ever use the phrase *The Devil made me do it!* She was the first female. Ever. If *you* think you feel alone, just imagine how she felt!

It's hard to be first at anything, and it is definitely lonely at the top. Think of Eve's situation: no other women had ever been born. There was no backyard fence to gossip over, no friend she could call and complain to, no white sales and no Minute Rice. Life in the Garden of Eden was idyllic, to be sure, until Eve made a decision to doubt what God had told her. That was her first mistake. Then the Garden of Eden became the Garden of Weedin' (literally!) and life (for all of us) took a downturn. All would have been lost, except for one thing: hope. God gave us all hope, and he used Eve to do it.

Before God created Eve, Adam had it made in the shade. He was independently wealthy, he didn't have to work hard, and he had the best house on the block. (The fact that it was the *only* house on the block simply put him in a more exclusive neighborhood.) Adam spent his days tending the Garden of Eden and in the evenings God paid him a personal visit and they walked the garden paths, talking together. Pretty nice life, right?

Adam didn't know it, but something was missing from this idyllic existence. There he was, minding his own business, exercising his creative genius by naming every bird, every tree, every bug, and every plant. (If you don't think he was a creative genius, you try coming up with a couple of million different

9

names! Adam was just enjoying life and enjoying God. But he really hit the mother lode when God brought Eve to him that day in the garden.

God knew Adam would need a companion, someone to share his life and make his happiness complete. Now, lest you think Eve was an afterthought, she wasn't. This woman was no Band-Aid fix that God decided to add later because he hadn't realized Adam would need a life's companion. God is God, and he doesn't do things halfway. Eve was *planned*. God was just waiting for Adam to be ready for her!

Just as Eve was no accident, neither are you. God planned you, too. He knew all about you when you were being formed in your mother's womb. Before time began, he knew everything that went into making you who you are, and he knew everything that was going to happen to you. (Don't take my word for it; check out Psalm 139.) He also knew Eve would commit the first sin: doubting what he had said and challenging the one rule he had given to her and Adam. He knew she would succumb to Satan's twisted reasoning. Eve waffled in her beliefs, she coveted the knowledge Satan offered her, and she screwed up. She wasn't satisfied with what God had provided for her and she wanted more. But God used her anyway c to bless all mankind. You and I wouldn't be here if it weren't for Eve.

Just as God knew what was going to happen, he knew what he was going to do about it. He loved Adam and Eve so much that he provided a way for them to be reconciled with himself. In Genesis 3:15 God promised a Redeemer who would make reconciliation and restoration between God and mankind possible. He forgave Adam and Eve, because he is God. And he provided a way to make things right again: faith in the Redeemer he promised to send in the future. Adam and Eve and all the men and women who lived up to the time the Redeemer was born on Earth looked forward to that Redemption act in faith.

Since the day that Redeemer sacrificed his life to pay the penalty for mankind's willful disobedience so we could be reconciled to God and rose from the dead so we could have abundant and eternal life, all the men and women who have ever lived have looked back to that Redemption act in faith.

Consider Eve in the light of all this: the first female, the first vegetarian homemaker, the first wife, the first mother, the first sinner, the first woman to repent, the first woman to trust her eternal fate to the Redeemer whom God promised to provide. The first woman in everything. What a giant of the faith she was! What a wonderful example of hope and trust she is to us.

Just try to put yourself in Eve's place for a minute. Here she was — a screaming kid named Cain on her hip, trying to gather enough berries to make shortcake for dessert, and no Bisquick in the house! No disposable diapers, either. The goat had to be milked, the beans had to be snapped, the chickens had to be fed and Adam was out tinkering around in the garden, as usual. On top of all that, she was pregnant with her second son, Abel. I don't know about you, but I can really empathize with Eve! She had it all, and then she lost it all. But God blessed her beyond belief anyway, because she put her trust in him.

God gave Adam and Eve the freedom of choice, and they made the wrong one. He gave us that freedom of choice, as well. Don't make the wrong one! We must choose where we will spend eternity, and what kind of life we will live while we are on Earth. Eve made it into God's Hall of Fame, in spite of the fact that she screwed up, because she placed her faith in God and believed the impossible. If God could use a screw-up like Eve to bless all mankind, he can use you, too. You only have to ask him.

Sarah

Trouble In The Bedroom
(or Where's The Viagra When You Need It?)

Abraham's wife Sarah was drop-dead gorgeous — a real babe! But she was barren, which was a real reproach in that day. The stigma of not having children put Sarah under tremendous personal pressure. To add to her problems, she and her husband lived with her father-in-law, Terah. Alzheimer's hadn't been discovered yet, but Sarah could probably relate to those of us who end up caring for an aged parent. (Of course, at this point, at age seventy-five, Abraham wasn't exactly a teenager, either.)

God had spoken to Abraham and promised that he would be the father of a great nation. He was overjoyed! He reasoned that to be a father of a great nation, he would have to have at least one son and a great many descendants. Obviously he couldn't do that alone. He needed Sarah, and she couldn't have children. Part of God's promise was that Abraham and Sarah were to launch out on their own, specifically to leave his father's house and go to a land which God would show him.

It's a good guess that Abraham's dad had something to say about this plan of his son's to leave home because when Abraham and Sarah left, not only did Terah go with them, he took his grandson, Lot, along as well. This was not exactly what God had told Abraham to do, and it caused some problems. It was incomplete obedience on Abraham's part.

So here was Sarah, sixty-five years old, still beautiful, without a home to call her own, living in a tent with an old husband who had gone completely off his rocker! Genesis 12:5 says, "and they went forth to go into the land of Canaan; and into the land of Canaan they came." There was a heap of living between points A and B!

Put yourself in Sarah's sandals. God had instructed Abraham to go west toward the Mediterranean, so every afternoon the sun was in their eyes. The city of Ur was at sea level, and Canaan was about 800 miles due west. Because they couldn't get enough traction in the shifting sand dunes of the Syrian Desert, they had to leave the RV back home in Ur of the Chaldees and travel by camel. Day after day, they plodded through the burning sands, setting up camp every night, breaking camp every morning, and climbing hills up to 3,000 feet high. It might have been a fun trip if it had been just her and Abraham, but the whole family was along, including every dog, cat, kid and servant. They even had all their furniture, including that ratty old recliner Abraham refused to part with. Sarah was *not* a happy camper

By the time they finally arrived in Canaan, there was a famine in full swing. This was a real test of Abraham's faith. He couldn't see how God was going to make him the father of a great nation if he died of hunger, so to help God out, he took his family to Egypt to live, where there was plenty to eat. God had not told Abraham to go to Egypt at all, so he was running ahead of God's plan. Abraham learned that it never pays to try to help God live up to his promises, because God doesn't need our help and he doesn't make promises he doesn't intend to keep.

When the family arrived in Egypt, Abraham was afraid the Egyptians would see how beautiful Sarah was and would kill him in order to have her. So he decided to tell a half-truth and say that Sarah was his sister, and he instructed her to say the same. In a way, it was the truth. She was, indeed, his half-sister, but they were also married — a little fact they neglected to mention. People did notice Sarah, and before too long, she came to the attention of Pharoah himself. Because of this deception, Abraham ended up a guest at the palace, and Sarah ended up in Pharoah's harem. Pharoah treated Abraham very well, giving him great wealth and many servants. After all, nothing was too good for Sarah's brother. While he was living it up, enjoying the pleasures of life, Abraham was unwittingly throwing obstacles in the way of God's plan for his life. With Sarah living in the harem, just how exactly was she supposed to get pregnant by Abraham? These two giants of the faith had an imperfect faith and an imperfect understanding, so they kept getting in God's way. They soon learned, however, that Pharoah's palace was not the place of blessing for them. God protected Sarah in that none of the Egyptians slept with her, but he sent plagues on the Egyptians and revealed to Pharoah the reason for them. Pharoah called Abraham onto the palace carpet and sent both him and Sarah away, along with all the gifts he had given them. However, ill-gotten gain is never a blessing. They had camels full of souvenirs from their trip to Egypt and they had to return to square one — right back where they had started. But this time, there were a lot of unbelievers in Abraham's household that had been added in Egypt. Abraham learned that running ahead of God always brings consequences. He also learned that a half-truth is also a half-lie. That's not an option with God.

The strife in Abraham's household increased to the point where no one could live with it. Abraham offered Lot his choice of land for his very own, and sent him and his side of the family away. Lot was shrewd, if he wasn't anything else, and he chose the best land for himself, to the east — the beautiful well-watered plains of Jordan — and settled in the suburbs of a city named Sodom. (The Bible says it was a sin city of the worst kind.)
Abraham, however, stayed in Canaan, the place of blessing. God told Abraham to look in all four directions and renewed his promise to give all the land he could see to his descendants. This time, Abraham didn't try to help God out. He packed up Sarah and all the animals, the servants and their furniture and settled in Hebron. It was a good move.

Meanwhile, Abraham was getting older by the minute and so was Sarah. Ten years after God had first promised Abraham a son, Sarah was more convinced than ever that Abraham must be nuts, expecting her to get pregnant at age seventy-five! (Abraham was now eighty-five.) One day Abraham asked God, "Where's that son you promised me? Am I supposed to leave everything to my servant Eliezer who was born in my house? Is he

14

my heir?" God again reaffirmed his promise for a son to be born to Abraham and Sarah. More time went on. Finally, Sarah couldn't wait another minute. Forgetting the lessons of the past, she suggested that Abraham take her Egyptian maid, Hagar, as his second wife and have a child by her. Sarah reasoned that since she owned Hagar, the child would be hers and God's promise would be fulfilled. Sarah was depending on her human understanding and was tired of waiting for some great miracle. At seventy-six, Sarah was just plain tired of waiting. So she decided to help God out — again. (Some people never learn.)

Abraham went along with Sarah's plan, and Hagar gave birth to Ishmael when Abraham was eighty-six years old. (Can't you just see him tottering to the Little League games now?) Sarah thought the birth of Ishmael settled everything. This foolishness of her getting pregnant was over once and for all. Unfortunately, everyone had to live with the consequences of Sarah's wrong decision for the rest of their lives. God told Abraham that Ishmael would be a problem child — wild and against every man. The years ahead would be full of trouble, and they had no one to blame but themselves. (The world is still living with Sarah's wrong choices.)

When Abraham turned ninety-nine and Sarah was eighty-nine, Ishmael was thirteen. That was when God once again renewed his promise to Abraham that he would have a son with Sarah. That would be the child God had promised. Abraham reacted just like any man: he fell down laughing! He was rolling on the floor at the absurdity of the situation. "Come on, God! Sarah's going to give birth at ninety? Let's just use Ishmael, okay?"

God's answer was that Abraham was to name the new baby Isaac. God reminded him that he had promised Abraham a son with Sarah, not Hagar, and advised him to get ready for the pitter-patter of little feet because Isaac would be born in nine months.

Not too long after that, Abraham and Sarah had unex-pected guests. Abraham saw three men coming toward his home, and he just knew there was something special about them. He ran to meet them and invited them for dinner. Sarah couldn't believe her ears! Can't you just hear her now? "Isn't that just great. Three more mouths to feed. Would someone like to tell me how I'm supposed to stretch the meatloaf?" Abraham (trying to be helpful) suggested pancakes with veal scaloppini. (It's true! He did. Check out Genesis 18:6 and 8 if you don't believe me.)

After the meal, Sarah was standing in the doorway of the tent, watching and listening to the three men talking with her husband. They reaffirmed that Sarah would give birth to a son in nine months. Now Sarah had not only already been through menopause, she was ninety years old. The Bible describes her as well stricken in age. Perhaps she had a touch of arthritis and her skin was wrinkled from the constant sun of the desert; maybe she was a little bent over. When she heard them say she'd give birth in nine months, she reacted exactly as you and I would have. She laughed to herself. "This is really rich! I'm supposed to enjoy a night of sexual ecstasy with a 100-year old man? Give me a break!" (Where's the Viagra when you need it???)

It is widely believed among Bible scholars that one of the three men was actually the Son of God. He knew her thoughts, even though she had not spoken out loud, and he asked Abraham, "Why did Sarah laugh? She will have a son." That shut Sarah's mouth. Sarah denied laughing, because she was afraid. Not only was it rude by their standards of hospitality, but she, too, had recognized the Lord in her spirit. The Lord said to her, "Yes, you did laugh." There are no secrets from God. Not then, and not now. When Abraham was an even 100 years old and Sarah was ninety, she did give birth to Isaac. Want to know her first question? "Should I breast-feed?" Just picture it: A ninety-year old woman knitting booties, living through morning sickness, giving birth to her first son, and then dealing with piles of dirty diapers and a fussy baby cutting teeth! She finally got what she had wanted all her life. And she had the grace to laugh at herself for doubting God's promise. She admitted God knew best and was in control of her life. (God probably breathed a big sigh of relief and said, "Finally!")

Sarah's problem was that her God was too small. We often fall into the same pothole. We need to give up and let God be God. He was (and is) capable of so much more than we can even imagine. He wants to delight us with surprises and fill our humdrum daily lives with miracle after miracle. Each of us has to give up running her own life, and let him guide us on the path that is best for us. Sarah finally learned that lesson. She enjoyed watching Isaac grow into a fine young man with children of his own. She died at the age of 127. (Abraham, however, was still going strong. and lived to be 175.) The lesson we learn from Sarah is plain: Don't run ahead of God or try to help him keep his promises by giving premature birth to Ishmaels. Wait for God's perfect timing in your life, and you will have the best he has planned for you.

Hagar
The Other Wife

Before Sarah gave birth to Isaac, she had suggested that Abraham marry her Egyptian maid, Hagar, and have a son with her. Abraham did that, and lived to regret it. So did Sarah. When Hagar's son, Ishmael, was born, Hagar had something she could hold over Sarah's head and she played her advantage for all it was worth.

We don't know what kind of servant Hagar was, except that she did as her mistress told her. Hagar made the 800-mile trip back to Canaan as Sarah's maid. Think what that meant. Every time Sarah wanted a drink, or had to blow her nose, Hagar was the one who had to fetch and carry. There were no jets, no Amtrak, no air-conditioned van with cup holders for every passenger and a VCR to entertain the kids. Every night Hagar had to help set up Sarah's tent and make sure she had everything she wanted for her comfort. And every morning she had to help break camp and make sure nothing got left behind. Hagar's life was not easy, by any means!

If Hagar was anything, she was an opportunist. When Sarah's lack of faith that God would give her a son at her advanced age of seventy-six spawned the idea of Abraham's having a son with Sarah's maid, it seemed like a logical choice. Hagar, however, was in her prime and saw this as her ticket to a better life. The minute she knew she was pregnant, she began to look down on Sarah and have contempt for her. (*Ha, ha! I'm pregnant and you're not!*) Hagar pressed her advantage and flaunted her good fortune, rubbing Sarah's nose in it every chance she got. Finally, Sarah had had enough of Hagar's supercilious smirk and complained to Abraham. "My wrong be upon you," she wailed. "It's your problem now. Do something about it!" Abraham (typical man as he was) washed his hands of the whole situation and threw it right back at Sarah, telling her to do whatever she wanted to. "She's still your maid. You take care of it!" So Sarah vented her frustration, resentment and anger on Hagar. She treated her so badly, Hagar ran away. There she was, pregnant, coping with morning sickness, unemployment, and homelessness, wandering around the desert alone.

This was not good, and God did something about it. He knew Sarah had been unfair and he sent an angel to care for Hagar and her unborn child. The angel found her sitting by a watering hole in the wilderness, and called her by name. (Remember that Hagar was not of Abraham's faith; she was Egyptian. For God to send an angel to speak directly to her was a minor miracle.) The angel asked Hagar how she had gotten to this point in her life, and where she was going. Imagine Hagar's shock and surprise that this angel knew her and was concerned about her! She told him she was running away from her mistress, and the angel told her to return to Sarah and submit herself to her mistress' authority. That was exactly what Hagar did not want to do. It was too humiliating. Sometimes, when we try to take things into our own hands, or try to squirm out of a difficult situation, that is the very thing we need to do — humble ourselves, so God can lift us up in his own timing.

The angel promised Hagar that she would give birth to a son whom she should name Ishmael and that he would become the father of a great nation, too many people to number. Hagar's wilderness experience changed her life forever. It was a watershed experience. She went back to Sarah, and (as far as we know) she changed her ways. We are not told any more about her in the Scriptures. She was probably a good maid, and good for Sarah, as well as a good mother to Ishmael.

For thirteen years, Ishmael was Abraham's only son, and he must have loved him dearly. That must have made Hagar happy. From Ishmael came the twelve sons whose descendants became what we now call the Arab world. From Sarah's son, Isaac, born thirteen years after Ishmael, came the twelve tribes of Israel. And now you know why the Arab and Jewish people have had such a stormy history. It all started when Sarah and Abraham tried to help God fulfill his promise of an heir.

From Hagar we learn that if we submit ourselves to God's plan for our lives, he will care for us, provide for us, and give us riches and blessings beyond measure. We need to give him our co-operation, and be willing to do as he tells us to, even if it doesn't make sense to us.

How do you know when it's God who is telling you to do something? You have to be on speaking terms with him, so you can recognize his voice. If you have given your heart to him, he will talk with you. Put aside a few minutes and get quiet before him. Empty your mind and just wait, expecting him to speak to you. Don't ask him for anything; just listen. Sometimes that is the hardest thing of all to do! Susannah Wesley, mother of John and Charles Wesley, had seventeen children. When she wanted to find time alone with God, she sat down and threw her apron over her head. All her children knew not to interrupt her when she had her apron over her head, because she was listening to God. If she could find time to be alone with him, you can, too. Tomorrow morning when you wake up, try leaning your elbows on the windowsill of the day and simply telling God you love him. He will respond. He cannot resist being loved any more than you or I can.

Lot's Wife
If Looks Could Kill!

We're not told much about Lot's wife, but we can learn a very important lesson from her. Since we don't even know her name, let's call her Lottie.

Abraham had provided well for his nephew, Lot, and his family. He had set him up in business as a cattle rancher. When it came time for Abraham and Lot to go their separate ways, Abraham had given Lot first choice of the land. He chose to live in the suburbs of Sodom — a name that has come to mean the epitome of wickedness — filled with debauchery, murder, thievery, the riches of the world and a total disregard for God.

Lot had done very well for himself, and the entire family was used to having the best the world had to offer. They were suburbanites, titillated by the pleasures and comforts of the world — a portrait of spiritual immaturity, with little room for God in their lives. Lottie enjoyed every privilege, complete with a closet full of the very finest designer fashions and more sandals than Imelda Marcos! She had it all, and reveled in her life as a wealthy suburban cattle baron's wife. No car-pooling or housework for this gal!

We aren't told how much or how little influence Lottie had on the choices her husband made, but it's probably safe to assume she wielded a lot of influence. Life was good, but that was about to change.

Without much warning, war broke out among the local tribes and Lot was captured, along with all his family and servants and possessions. Abraham heard about Lot's kidnapping,

21

armed 318 of his servants and took this SWAT team to rescue Lot and bring him home. Lot was lucky that time. But God had finally had enough of Sodom and told Abraham he was going to destroy the city, because its sin was so very great.

Abraham interceded and pleaded with God to not destroy the righteous people in the city. God finally agreed to not destroy any righteous people, even if there were only ten. And to keep his word, he sent two angels to warn Lot. (No, they weren't named Monica and Tess!) Lot saw the angels coming and went to meet them, inviting them to stay with him for the night. Just before they all went to bed, Lot's house was surrounded by the men of Sodom, demanding that Lot turn the two angels (who had taken the form of men) over to them. They planned to gang rape them and then kill them. Lot went out to plead with the group to not do this terrible thing. And he offered the would-be rapists his own two unmarried daughters who were living at home in place of the men. This was *not* Lot's finest hour.

The angels pulled him back in and caused the group of men to be blind. Then they warned Lot of the impending destruction and told him to take his entire family and possessions and get out of town immediately. There was no time to waste.

Shaking in his sandals, Lot told his sons-in-law who refused to believe him. They thought he was off his rocker and chose not to go with him. Life for them was just fine as it was. So the angels told Lot to take just his wife and two unmarried daughters living at home and go.

How long would *you* hesitate in a case like this? Believe it or not, Lot dragged his feet. He looked around at all he would be leaving behind. He focused on the past and what he would be losing. Finally, one angel took Lot by the hand and the other angel took Lottie by the hand and they each took one of the daughters and physically led the four of them out of the city to safety, beyond the area to be destroyed.

God was very merciful to Lot. His instructions had been to escape with their lives and "Don't look behind you!" He told Lot to go to the mountain or he would be caught in the destruction that was coming to the low land. Basically, he told Lot to get to higher ground.

Just get a grasp here on the situation. Life as Lot knew it was about to come screaming down on his head. Only the four members of his immediate family were being spared. So what did Lot do? Did he take charge and get his family to safety? Did he obey God in gratitude for his life being spared? No! He stood there and argued with him! He begged God to let him go to Zoar (ZOH-are) a small nearby city, instead,. He actually said he was afraid to go to higher ground because something bad might happen to him and he might die! What a wimp!! The God of the Universe was promising to protect him and there was Lot, refusing to believe him with only minutes to spare before he'd lose his life. There's a lesson here for us. We, too, have a choice. We can choose to either live in fear, or believe God's promises and go to higher ground.

In this decisive moment, that defining turning point of his life, Lot chose second best. In his mercy, God kept his promise to Abraham and saved Lot's life anyway, allowing him to go to Zoar instead of to the mountain. But God's disappointment must have been deep.

Lot got what he wanted, but he showed his true colors. His life was spared and he was allowed to preserve a semblance of his lifestyle, but it was not God's *best* choice for him. Lot didn't want to give up his comfortable life. He counted the cost of following God and decided it was too high. Can you imagine the leanness in Lot's soul for the rest of his life, knowing he had made a poor choice? Trying to keep one foot in the world and one foot in God's will never works to our advantage.

Where was Lottie during all this wheeling and dealing with God? We aren't told specifically what her feelings were on the matter, but it was almost surely *not* her will to leave her powerful life in Sodom behind. It's a safe supposition because of what Lottie did as they were being led out of the city by the angels. She looked back at what she was leaving behind, and she was turned into a pillar of salt. (I can hear you: Yeah, right!)

Preposterous? Not at all, when you check out the meaning of the Hebrew word used in the Scriptures. This was not a lovely crystal shaker of Morton's table salt we're talking about. We're told that fire and brimstone rained down on the city, much as would happen in a volcanic eruption. Archaeologists have uncovered victims of the eruption of Mt. Vesuvius whose bodies were preserved and petrified when they were caught in the volcanic ash and heat. The essence of the Hebrew word used here for salt means *to rub to pieces or pulverize, to disappear as dust or vanish away.*

Likewise, the meaning of the Hebrew word translated *looked back* sheds light on what kind of look that really was. When Lottie looked back, she didn't just glance over her shoulder quickly and keep on following Lot out of the city. The word means *to scan or look intently at*; by implication, it means *to regard with pleasure, favor or care.* That look Lottie allowed herself was filled with longing — for what she was losing and what she was being forced to leave behind. That look carried resentment, anger, fear of the future, and distrust. To put it bluntly, Lottie loved her stuff more than she loved God. She wasn't willing to leave what she had in order to get something better.

The lesson for us is clear: God cannot give us something better if we are clinging to the past. We have to walk away from it all: daily failures, fear of the future, friends who drag us down, little successes, enjoyable lifestyle, and whatever we think we've accomplished in life. Faithless Lottie couldn't move ahead because she was stuck in the past. As the saying goes, she wasn't worth her salt.

In Matthew 5:13 Jesus said to his followers, "You are the salt of the earth." The trouble with salt is, it doesn't do anyone any good until it gets out of the shaker. In order to move *ahead*, you must move *away* from something. It will probably be hard to do. But God has promised that the blessings will far outweigh the difficulties of following him. He'll walk with you every step of the way. He'll even pick you up and carry you over the worst spots. Just relax in his arms and let him do it.

Rebekah
Waiting For Mr. Right

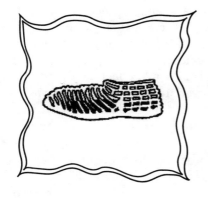

When his son Isaac was old enough, Abraham sent his servant back to his homeland to find the young man a wife and bring her back to him.

The servant, Eliezer (ell-ee-A-zar), prepared the camels for the journey and traveled to the city of Nahor in Mesopotamia. He arrived at suppertime. He had his tired, hot, dusty and thirsty camels kneel down by the village well where all the local women came to get their supply of water. Eliezer asked God to help him and prayed that to whomever he would say, "Put your pitcher down so I may have a drink," if that was the right woman for Isaac, she would offer to give *all ten* of his camels water also. This was no small miracle he was asking for! A camel can drink gallons and gallons of water, storing it up for when there might not be any. The woman who was foolish enough to offer to do this would have to make dozens and dozens of trips to the well to water just one camel. Now multiply that times ten. Why did Eliezer take ten camels? Because he had faith that God would find a bride for Isaac and he'd need the camels to bring back all her things. Eliezer wasn't trying to make things difficult. He was just trying to be very sure he got the right woman.

Before he finished the prayer, Rebekah arrived at the well. (God has promised that even before we ask, he will answer. Here's proof.) She filled her pitcher and was on her way home, balancing it on her shoulder. Eliezer watched her carefully and liked what he saw. He ran to her and asked her for a drink.

Rebekah didn't say, "Why should I?" She showed him

respect, just as *you* would if a well-dressed man showed up at your door with ten camels and asked for a drink. All the time Eliezer was drinking, he no doubt was thinking, "Is this the one?" He took his sweet time with that long, cool drink of water on a hot, dry day. Would she offer to water the camels? He was holding his breath when she did just that. He marveled as she not only gave the camels water, but also emptied her pitcher and ran again and again and again until all ten of them were satisfied. Amazing!!! There she was, this knockout beauty who was not only generous, but also gracious, kind, hospitable, patient and not afraid to work. If there was ever a "Perfect Ten", it was Rebekah. The Bible says she was even a virgin — qualified in every way to marry Isaac. (I'm not sure how he knew that, so we won't even go *there*!) But Eliezer didn't tip his hand until she was finished watering the camels.

Can you imagine what the other people thought as they watched this scene? Here's this sweet young thing making a bazillion trips, back and forth, up and down (and the *up* was with a heavy, full pitcher of water.) It's one thing to offer a glass of water to one thirsty person. It's an entirely different matter to quench the thirst of ten camels that have been on the road all day. Rebekah was no dummy. She knew what her offer meant in terms of effort. She knew what it would cost her to do this. No wonder Eliezer watched her in amazement.

Such commitment deserved a reward, and Eliezer gave her a gold earring and two gold bracelets. Remember that Eliezer's master, Abraham, was a very wealthy man — nothing but the best of everything — and Eliezer was in charge of it all. He had the power to give her whatever she deserved. When she accepted his gifts, he had the audacity to ask if he and his entire caravan could stay overnight at her father's home. Rebekah told him who her father was, and that there was plenty of room in their stables for all the camels and plenty of food for all of them as well. As it happened, Rebekah was a relative of Abraham's. She was actually Isaac's second cousin. God answered Eliezer's prayer to the smallest detail, above and beyond whatever he could have dreamed or hoped. (He'll do the same for you. Check out Ephesians 3:20.)

Just for a minute, put yourself in Rebekah's mother's sandals. You are, just finished feeding the family, dishes are done, getting ready to sit down and put your feet up and read the paper — and your kid shows up with an unexpected dinner guest who wants to stay over. And he just happens to have ten camels and camel-tenders who also need a meal and a place to sleep! How'd you like to clean up after *that* bunch in the morning?

What was Eliezer's reaction to all this? He bowed down and worshipped God, saying, "The Lord led me." Then he told Rebekah and her family that Abraham was his master and had sent him to find a bride for his son and heir, Isaac. (Suddenly, Rebekah's mom wasn't so tired anymore.)

Can you imagine Rebekah's family sitting around the dining room table listening to this incredible story of Eliezer's? When her parents agreed to let her marry Isaac, Eliezer gave Rebekah a bridal shower to end all bridal showers. Jewelry and a designer-label trousseau came out of those camels' saddlebags by the armloads. He also gave many gifts to the other members of her family.

The next morning, he was packing up and Rebekah's brother (Laban) and her mother asked if she could stay at least ten days. Eliezer said no, but left the choice up to Rebekah. Recognizing a good thing when she saw it, she said, "I'll go." She believed that since God had chosen Isaac for her, everything would work out. She committed. And trusted. Just so, when God reveals his plan for your life, you can commit and trust with all your heart.

Just before she left, Rebekah's family gave her this blessing, "Be thou the mother of thousands of millions." They were referring, of course, to God's promise to Abraham that he would be the father of a great nation — the descendants of Isaac and Rebekah. Then the entire caravan left for Abraham's place.

Days later, as they drew near their destination, Isaac was out walking in the field, meditating. He saw them coming. (Ten camels raise a lot of dust on the horizon.) He set out to meet them, eager to meet his bride-to-be. Isaac wasn't the only one watching the horizon. Rebekah saw him coming and asked Eliezer who it was. When she learned it was Isaac, she got off her camel and went to meet the man of her dreams. He took her home, married her, and (best of all) fell in love with her. When Abraham died at age 175, Isaac inherited his entire estate. Rebekah was a rich woman, in every way. (When it's right, it's *right*!)

What lesson can we gain from Eliezer's declaration, "I, being in the way, the Lord led me?" Anyone who drives knows that it's easier to steer a moving car than one that's sitting still. If you're trying to decide in which direction to move, and you're waiting for God to hit you over the head with a two-by-four, get out of park and get into gear! Get moving in the direction that *seems* right to you, but give God permission to steer you in the correct direction or turn you completely around. Tell him, "I think this is what you want me to do (or whom you want me to date, or whatever), so I'm going to move in this direction. But if this is *not* what you want, God, it's okay with me for you to lead me a different way." In James 1:5, God says if you don't know what to do, he'll tell you if you ask. Don't be afraid of missing his will. If you do, he'll come looking for you and correct your course if your attitude is right.

What if Rebekah had responded to Eliezer's request for a drink of water with, "I'm tired. Get it yourself!" She would have kicked herself the rest of her life. You never know when an Eliezer is going to knock on your door. In the Living Bible, Jeremiah 29:11 is paraphrased this way: "I know the plans I have for you, says the Lord — plans to give you a future and a hope." It's far better to wait and let God choose the right husband for you (or job, or friend) than to pick the wrong one for yourself. Determine right now not to settle for second best. Hold out for God's plan for your life. It's a good one!

Leah and Rachel

Cheaper By The Dozen

Rebekah and Isaac had twin sons, named Jacob and Esau. Esau, born first, should have had the blessings of his position. Rebekah, however, played favorites, and she loved Jacob best. When Isaac was old, almost blind, and near death, she conspired with Jacob. She tricked Isaac into bestowing the blessings of the first-born on him, rather than on Esau, to whom they rightly belonged. This was a problem, of course — as soon as Esau discovered what had happened, it drove a wedge between the brothers that never really went away. Esau hated Jacob and planned to kill him. Rebekah overheard him talking about it and warned Jacob. She sent him to stay with his uncle, her brother Laban, telling Jacob she'd send for him when the situation calmed down.

Rebekah and Isaac didn't really like Judith, Esau's wife, because she was a foreigner. (Strange isn't it, that we exactly have the same prejudices today? We really haven't learned a lot, have we?) Rebekah worried that Jacob would also marry outside the fold and fretted that then her life would be for nothing. Isaac commanded Jacob to marry someone related to Rebekah's brother, Laban, so the blessing of Abraham could stay in the family. (This is the same blessing that should have been Esau's by birthright.)

On the way to live with his Uncle Laban, Jacob camped overnight just off the road. He didn't have much with him, because he had left under cover, in fear for his life, so he used a flat rock for a pillow that night. He had a vivid dream. (Hard rocks don't make for soft sleep!) In the dream, God blessed him and confirmed that he would be the one through whom God would bless all the peoples of the Earth. When he awoke, he turned the rock pillow on end and poured oil on it to commemorate what had happened to him there. He made a vow to be 100% committed to God, and to give 10% of all his wealth to God as well.

When Jacob arrived in Laban's town, he saw his cousin Rachel (Laban's younger daughter), and fell head over heels in love with her. He helped her roll the stone cover off the well and helped her water her father's sheep. Then he kissed her, and told her who he was. (Didn't waste much time, did he?) She ran and told her father and together they went to get Jacob and brought him home with them. Jacob told the family the entire story of why he was there. He stayed for a month and helped out at Laban's sheep ranch.

At the end of the month, Laban offered to pay Jacob for his work and asked what he wanted for wages. By this time, not only was Jacob in love with Rachel, but Rachel was also in love with him, so he offered to work for Laban for free for a period of seven years if he could have Rachel for his wife at the end of that time. Laban agreed. Time loses its meaning, when you're in love, and the seven years seemed to fly by for the young couple. When Jacob announced it was time for them to get married, Laban threw a huge wedding party for them. But when it was time to go to bed, Laban sent Leah, his older daughter — who was not as pretty as Rachel — to Jacob's tent. Jacob had probably had a great deal of wine at the party, and since it was the custom for the women to wear veils over their faces, it's understandable that Jacob was not aware just exactly who was waiting for him in the marriage bed.

Can you imagine how angry Rachel must have been at being kept from her own wedding, and then to discover the trick her father had played on her and Jacob? Worse yet, Jacob was now officially married to her sister! (Sounds like one of today's soap operas, doesn't it? In fact, I think I saw that episode....) You and I wouldn't have put up with that situation for one second. Today's woman would have gone to Jacob's tent and punched Leah's lights out! But the law of the land back then was that the older daughter had to be married first, and Laban was well aware that he would have a hard time marrying off not-so-pretty Leah.

The next morning, Jacob woke up, slightly hung over and bleary-eyed, but not so bleary-eyed that he didn't realize what had happened. He took a good look at the woman he had slept with and went storming in to his father-in-law. Laban explained the custom of marrying off the older daughter first, and promised Jacob if he'd give Leah his undivided attention for a week, at the end of seven days he could marry Rachel as well. But he'd have to work for Laban for another seven years to pay for Rachel. So Leah had Jacob all to herself for a week, and then the woman who *should* have been his wife moved in.

That must have been some week in Laban's household. Playing second fiddle wasn't Rachel's style. She was used to all the attention and having things her way. Leah had learned the hard way that if you aren't the lead dog, the scenery never changes. Can't you just imagine she played that week for all it was worth? It must have driven Rachel nuts to think about Jacob sleeping with Leah every night of that week — in her place! How would you have liked to sit down to dinner every night in *that* family?

At the end of the week, Jacob and Rachel were married. Tension must have crackled in the air like electricity when Rachel and her maid moved in. Now Jacob was living with *four* women, because Leah had her maid with her, too. And every single one of them knew that Jacob loved Rachel best.

Put yourself in Leah's shoes. She knew she couldn't hold a candle to Rachel's beauty, no matter how many times she exchanged her lipstick and eyeshadow at the local drugstore. But Leah had one thing going for her, and in that arena, Rachel was a non-contender. Leah was very fertile, and she was forever having babies with Jacob while Rachel remained barren. After Leah had produced four healthy sons, Rachel had had her nose rubbed in it long enough. She went to Jacob and said, "If you don't get me pregnant, I'm going to die!" And Jacob, already driven to distraction with the tension in the household, got very angry. He yelled at Rachel, "There's nothing wrong with *my* plumbing! It's not my fault God has made you unable to have children!" Rachel stormed out of the room with murder in her eyes, and stormed back in with her maid. She used the same scheme Sarah had with Hagar. Rachel told Jacob to sleep with her maid so she could claim the children as her own. (Remember, the maid was Rachel's property, so she would, in effect, own the maid's offspring as well.) Rachel's maid had two sons by Jacob. Now there were four women, six little boys under ten running around the house — and Jacob. (For *this* he worked 14 years?)

The only woman in the house at this point who hadn't slept with Jacob was Leah's maid. (You guessed it!) Leah followed Rachel's lead and gave Jacob *her* maid as his wife, knowing that any children they had would be legally Leah's, and she'd have more children than Rachel. Pressing her advantage, when Leah's maid gave birth to a son, Leah named him Gad, which meant *troop*. (She wasn't kidding.) Then her maid had yet another son. (That made eight, in case you're keeping score.)

At this point, Reuben, Jacob's oldest son, discovered some mandrakes in a field and brought them home to his mother, Leah. (Mandrakes were a known aphrodisiac and Reuben thought he'd give her a helping hand.) When Rachel discovered the mandrakes, she asked Leah for some of them because she wanted to get pregnant. The two sisters made a deal. Rachel offered Leah a night of wedded bliss with Jacob in exchange for some of the love potion #9. Leah agreed. At the end of the day, Leah went to meet Jacob as he was coming home for dinner and informed him that he'd be sleeping with *her* that night because she had hired his services with some of Reuben's mandrakes. (What an ego Jacob must have had! All those women fighting over who was going to sleep with him which night!) As a result of that little deal, Leah had another son. And then she managed to have yet another one. Leah thought that surely Jacob would live in *her* wing of the house now because she had given him so many sons. (That's six for Leah, plus two from her maid and two for Rachel's maid.) She figured she had earned his love. However, it didn't work that way, because you cannot earn anyone's love. It's either there, or it isn't. And Jacob loved Rachel. We're never told that he loved Leah in the same way.

Meanwhile, back in Rachel's wing of the mansion, Jacob's favorite wife was beseeching God to even the score and give her a son of her own. The mandrakes must have worked their magic, because Rachel *finally* got pregnant and presented her husband with a beautiful son. They named him Joseph. Jacob was now the proud, if bedraggled, husband of four wives and the father of 11 sons. It's anybody's guess how many girls were born in between!

Jacob decided it was now time to leave Laban and head back to Isaac and Rebekah's homestead. When he told Laban he was leaving, that sly old fox asked him to stay, because he had figured out God had blessed him because of Jacob's presence. Laban virtually told Jacob to name his price, just stay. If there's one thing Jacob had learned through all this, it was patience. So he struck a deal with Laban that he would stay if he could have all the speckled and spotted cattle, sheep and goats from Laban's flocks. Laban agreed. And then he went out and removed all the ones he'd promised Jacob and moved them three-days' journey from Jacob. But patience wasn't the only thing Jacob had learned at Laban's ranch. He'd also become a shrewd businessman. When he discovered how he'd been cheated, he chose the strongest of Laban's flocks and separated them so they'd breed together, and using the awesome power of suggestion, put spotted and speckled twigs in front of them when they mated. When the strong, healthy offspring were born, he kept all the spotted and speckled ones for himself, giving Laban a taste of his own medicine. Jacob got wealthier and wealthier.

One day, he overheard Laban's sons talking about him and realized that his father-in-law's attitude had changed toward him. Living with his in-laws was no longer a good idea, so God gave Jacob the high sign that it was time to leave. When he presented the idea to Rachel and Leah, they readily agreed.

The trip back to the land of Jacob's birth was marked by four major events. First, Laban set out after him, caught up with him and they barely managed to avoid out-and-out battle by finally striking a peace agreement. To commemorate the event, they stacked up some rocks and agreed that Laban would forever stay on his side of the rock pile and Jacob would forever stay on the other side. It was there that Jacob pronounced what is often mistaken for a benevolent benediction, but was in reality a warning shot across Laban's bow: "The Lord watch between me and thee, when we are absent one from another." Translation: *Watch your step, Laban, you conniving old man. God's keeping his eye on you!*

The second thing that happened was that Jacob met some angels along the way and decided it was a sign that he should send Esau a message that he was arriving, rather than just showing up on the family doorstep. The messengers came right back and told Jacob that they met Esau and he was coming to meet his long-lost brother — with 400 men. Jacob knew this was no welcome-home-dear-brother party, and he was very afraid. Jacob divided up all the people with him — wives, servants, children — and all the herds of animals and sent them ahead to meet Esau in a long parade of homage and presents designed to appease Esau's anger. Jacob was the last one in the parade, and he was alone.

The third event, and perhaps the most important, was that once Jacob was alone, God appeared to him as a man that night and wrestled with him. We can infer that Jacob knew with whom he was struggling, because he refused to let the man go until he blessed him. It was at this point that Jacob came face-to-face with his God and his name was changed to Israel. The next day, he met Esau and his army. Jacob's appeasement tactics had worked. Esau's anger had abated and the two brothers struck an uneasy peace, which was maintained by their staying as far apart as possible. Esau returned home, and Israel (Jacob) built himself a house in a different location. (Smart move.)

This had all been hard on Jacob, but not as hard as the last major event that occurred after he settled into his new home. His beloved Rachel gave him another son, Benjamin, but she died in childbirth. We are told later that Jacob loved Benjamin best, because he was Rachel's last gift to him. Now Jacob, or Israel, had a full house, in every sense of the word — twelve sons to carry on his name and build the house of Israel. From these twelve men came the twelve tribes of Israel and, eventually, the country of Israel as we know it today. God did, indeed, keep his promise to Abraham and made him the father of a great nation.

The Israelites have a truly fascinating and extraordinary history, and many ups and downs in their relationship with God. It's interesting that the Bible always gives us both sides of the story, good and bad. Why did God do that? Because he's real, and he always tells it like it is. God was always there for Israel, whether they acknowledged him or not. He's always there for you, too, whether you believe he exists, or whether you think he exists but is too busy to care about your little upsets and situations in life. From God's dealings with the Israelites, and from his dealings with me, I can personally vouch for his existence and his great love for each and every one of his children. If you don't believe he loves you, ask him. Then be prepared, because he'll reveal himself and his love to you, and your life will never be the same! Guaranteed.

Jochebed and The Princess

What They Did For Love

When Jacob was a very old man, a famine struck the land. At the invitation of his son, Joseph, Jacob and his entire family (70 of them) moved to Egypt so Joseph could take care of them and provide for them. Joseph lived to be 110 years old, and by the time Joseph and his generation had died off, the children of Israel (Jacob's descendants) had been very prolific. The Bible says the land of Egypt was filled with Hebrews. The problem was that Egypt had a new pharoah, one who hadn't known Joseph, and he didn't like having so many Israelites in his country. The stage was set for a huge confrontation.

It all started when Pharoah enslaved the Hebrews and told them to build treasure cities for him. He set taskmasters over them to be sure they worked hard enough. But the harder they were on the Israelites, the more babies they had — the one thing Pharoah didn't want! (By the time the Israelite men got home from slaving in the hot sun all day you would have thought they'd be too tired to do anything but fall asleep. Apparently, those Israelite women were irresistible!) The taskmasters clamped down harder and harder, making the working conditions intolerable and making it almost impossible for them to reach their daily quotas. The number of Israelites increased year by year.

Finally Pharoah ordered the midwives who attended the Hebrew women to kill all the male babies born to the Hebrews. But the midwives feared the God of Israel and disobeyed Pharoah, telling him that the babies came out before the midwives even got there because the Hebrew women did everything quickly, even faster than the Egyptian women. Believe it or not, he bought their story, and God protected the midwives for honoring him. Pharoah's next edict was that every Egyptian was responsible for drowning all the male babies born to the Hebrews. Life for a Hebrew male infant was not looking good.

One day a son was born to Amram and Jochebed (JOCK-eh-bed) Levi. He was a beautiful healthy baby and Jochebed kept him hidden for three months. That took a lot of faith on her part, because she was risking her own life by disobeying Pharoah's order. What a three months that must have been! She must have known this was a very special child and that the call of God was on his life. When it was no longer possible to hide the child, she wove a little basket with a cover from papyrus grass. She covered the entire thing with mud and pitch — a watertight cocoon of protection. She believed God had a special plan for her son, and she was right.

Jochebed took the baby, the basket and her daughter, Miriam, and went down to the spot in the river where Pharoah's daughter and her maids went to bathe each day. She put her son in the basket, put the cover on it and, with a prayer, pushed it gently off in the direction of the princess, aiming for the best that life could offer. What faith this mother had! When the princess saw the little basket floating along the river's edge, she sent one of her maids to get it. She opened it, saw the beautiful child softly crying, realized he was a Hebrew and her heart went out to him. (He was a heart breaker from the very beginning.)

Jochebed wasn't the only female in the family with gumption. Miriam, the baby's sister, stepped forward and spoke to the princess. She offered to find a Hebrew wet nurse for her. The princess nodded her approval. Miriam was no dummy. She knew she was taking a risk to even offer to help. This baby was supposed to have been killed at birth. It was a stroke of divine humor that the daughter of the man who had ordered the baby killed was now going to be his adopted mother. This little Hebrew boy was going to be Pharoah's grandson! Miriam went and got the baby's (and her own) mother to nurse him for the princess. Jochebed had given the baby to God, and he gave him back to her. The princess paid her to do what she would have gladly done for love alone! Isn't that just like God? Children are one of His gifts to us, on loan for a short time. God entrusts them to our care and expects us to do whatever it takes to protect them, nurture them and raise them as godly men and women.

When the baby was weaned, Jochebed took him to the princess and she officially adopted him. By then, he had gotten a proper start in life from his birth mother. Of course it was hard for her to give him up. (She had to do that twice!) But the alternative was unacceptable. And God rewarded her faith.

It was very significant that the princess named her adopted son Moses, a distinctly Hebrew name. We do not know if she believed in the God of the Hebrews, but we do know that this woman made it her business to protect Moses' Hebrew heritage. We can infer that she also went out on a limb for this boy. All of a sudden she had a young son with a Hebrew name. This was very suspicious. The palace phone lines must have been humming with gossip! *Can you believe it? She has the audacity to bring that kid into Pharoah's family!! Oh, come on! She must have had an affair with one of the Hebrew slaves. Just wait until the King hears about this one!*

Yes, it cost the Egyptian princess plenty to raise her adopted son. But she was the daughter of the King of Egypt, and she knew her position would protect both her and her son. (She was probably the apple of her daddy's eye and could wrap him around her little finger.) This was a powerful woman and she used her influence to do the right thing. Where would Moses have been without her? Probably dead. God used this woman to alter the history of an entire race. She had integrity, compassion, a love of children, and an innate sense of justice. She did the politically incorrect, but morally right thing at her own risk. The entire Jewish population of the world owes her a debt of gratitude.

Two women — a birth mother and an adoptive mother — formed the life of this one man who became one of the most revered and respected men in the history of the world.

Zipporah

Turning A Wimp Into Mr. Macho

It was probably no picnic being married to Moses. He had been given his start in life in the home of his Hebrew parents with his sister, Miriam, and his older brother, Aaron. (Obviously, someone had managed to spare Aaron's life also, or he had been born before Pharoah's cruel edict, since he was three years older than Moses.)

Jochebed and Amram had no doubt taught him about God and his Hebrew heritage while they had him with them — for a few years at least, since in that culture children were weaned at a later age than we are accustomed to. (Forget DeMille's movie. The chances are good that Moses' early Hebrew training stayed in his memory.) Then Moses moved in with his adoptive mother, the daughter of Pharoah, where he was educated in the best schools and raised as an Egyptian prince in Pharoah's palace. With all the advantages he had been given, Moses had grown into a stunning example of manhood.

In Exodus 2:11, we read that Moses mingled with his brothers (the Hebrews) and saw the way they were treated. He also witnessed an Egyptian beating a Hebrew and the injustice of the Hebrews' situation overwhelmed him. But he was also very much aware of his position as Pharoah's adopted grandson, and the political immunity it afforded him. He thought he could get away with anything. He was cocky. Yet there was this innate sense of identity with the enslaved Hebrews.

When he saw the Egyptian hit the Hebrew, Moses looked this way and that and saw no witnesses. With the power of an avenging angel and the righteous indignation of a civil rights crusader, he took it upon himself to administer justice. He killed the Egyptian and buried his body in the sand. Remember, the Ten Commandments hadn't been given yet — nor any of the Hebrew law. It was his conscience that convicted Moses and made him hide what he had done. What he also did wrong was take matters into his own hands, instead of trusting God to straighten things out in his own time. Every time we do that, we just get in deeper.

The day after Moses murdered the Egyptian, he went out among the Hebrews again, saw two of them fighting and intervened. Their response knocked him for a loop. "Who made you a judge over us? Are you going to kill us as you killed the Egyptian yesterday?" He was afraid. The word finally got back to Pharoah and he ordered Moses' assassination. And Moses — cocky, self-assured, proud, invincible Moses — ran away.

Actually, Moses was a wimp. Numbers 12:3 says he was the meekest man in all Israel. He left everything and everyone behind and ran for his life. About 250 miles later, he stopped to rest beside a well in Midian. And there he met the love of his life.

There he was, exhausted by fear and by this horrendous flight from the scene of his crime. He was covered with dust and badly in need of a shower and shave. (No doubt, he was out of deodorant and had left his toothbrush back at the palace.) On the outside, he was no Prince Charming, nor on the inside. His life was in total chaos. He was emotionally and physically drained, and he had no hope for the future. He had forgotten who he was, had lost his job, his self-worth and his drive. Whatever age he was at this time, he was definitely having a mid-life crisis. What kind of impression do you think he made on the seven sisters who arrived at the well to draw water for their father's flocks? I don't know about you, but I probably wouldn't have given him a second glance.

Picture this: Here was this tired and dirty fugitive from justice and seven women with all their thirsty sheep baahing and bleating a cacophony of bedlam. Now add a rowdy bunch of shepherds trying to drive the women away from the well. (Gives a whole new meaning to meeting the handsome stranger across a crowded room some enchanted evening, doesn't it?)

Now Moses was nothing if he wasn't the champion of the underdog, and he helped the women. And he did it in record time, because when they got home, their father asked why they were home so early. They told him about Moses and he scolded them for not bringing the man home for dinner. They went back for him, and Moses not only stayed for dinner, he stayed forty years and married one of the sisters, Zipporah (zip-POOR-ah). Then he settled down to the dull, everyday life of a shepherd. The adopted grandson of the King of Egypt — ruler over a bunch of sheep. What a comedown!

As a Hebrew male, Moses would have been circumcised when he was just a few days old. This was the sign among the Hebrews of God's promise to them through the Abrahamic covenant. It was God's symbolic mark of ownership on his chosen people. Every Hebrew knew this and complied. Zipporah probably knew it, too, since she was a descendant of Abraham and his second wife, Keturah. She may not have been aware, however, of all that happened between God and Jacob, or what had happened with Joseph. She knew enough, though, to know that Moses wasn't living up to his potential, or honoring his God.

In the Bible, Egypt is a symbol of the world and its pleasures. Now there's nothing wrong with the good life, unless it takes your focus off God. Because Moses had been raised in Pharoah's palace, he knew all about the good life. He had had it all: wealth, position, designer clothes and a career path paved with gold. When God called Moses to serve him, he had one foot in the world and one on sacred ground. He was a half-hearted follower of God, what we would today call a *lukewarm Christian*. Zipporah knew this about her husband, and loved him anyway. For forty years Moses and his new family lived on the backside of the desert, tending sheep. That's what it looked like, but what was really happening was that Moses was in training for the job of his life. What do you suppose he was thinking about day after day? Don't you imagine he was thinking about all that had happened to him and was trying to attach some meaning to it?

Then one day, Moses led his flock to the backside of the desert near Mt. Horeb — and met God face to face. Sometimes we meet God in the most unlikely places! You *expect* to meet him in a beautiful cathedral, or at a spiritual conference with thousands of people who love him. But God doesn't work the way people expect him to. We have to be careful not to try to put God in a little box and confine him to doing things the way we think he should.

Moses had an epiphany in the desert. An angel appeared to him in a flame of fire coming out of the middle of a bush. Was it a mirage? The bush was burning with fire, but it wasn't burning up. He decided to check it out and as he drew closer, the voice of God spoke to him from the bush. The rest is history. Moses' life was changed forever — and so was his wife's.

That night when he got home he told Zipporah, "Honey, a funny thing happened to me on the way to work this morning" (Exodus 4:20). He told her about the call of God on his life and that he was supposed to go back to Egypt and lead the Hebrews to their promised land. And he wanted her and the children to travel over 200 miles through the desert, back to the scene of his crime, on the back of a jackass! (If that had been me, my first reaction would have been that's what *he* was!) But luckily for Moses, Zipporah was a good match for him and she knew this man needed to get his priorities straightened out. If he didn't, nothing would ever be right for her husband again. She agreed to go.

One night they had checked in at a little motel on the way and God met with Moses again. The meeting nearly killed Moses. He had neglected the one thing God had commanded his people to do as a sign of his covenant with Israel: Moses had not circumcised his son. Moses had not done right by his son in ignoring it. It was also in direct disobedience to God. Zipporah was aware of this and she knew that, even though her husband had been called by God to do this great thing for his people, he was not giving God 100%. So she circumcised their son herself. She put on the figurative pants in the family and shamed Moses into doing what he should have done in the first place. It was a drastic step, but it worked. It shook Moses out of his lethargy and he finally took charge and became the fearless leader he was meant to be. But it took the love and commitment of a strong woman to do it.

God doesn't bless half-hearted commitment. He gave us his very best when he sent his only Son to die in our place. How can we give anything less than 100% back to him?

Miriam

Jealousy In The Camp

Miriam showed leadership tendencies early in her life when she had the boldness to approach Pharoah's daughter and suggest she find a wet nurse for the Hebrew baby boy the Princess had found floating on the river. God had given Miriam many gifts. She was not only a leader of women, she was also a musician, a dancer, a poet and a lover of God. Unfortunately, when you're extremely gifted, everyone tells you so. If you're not careful, a superiority complex can set in. Miriam, it seems, was susceptible to this temptation.

By the time we meet Miriam as an adult, she was sometimes full of herself, instead of being full of God. She thought she was quite a woman, and her position of leadership went to her head. She also had a judgmental attitude. For example, she didn't like Moses' wife, Zipporah, because she was from Ethiopia (*the land of burnt faces*) and was either very dark-skinned or black (Numbers 12:3). In disliking Zipporah, Miriam showed her own true colors.

Miriam was also known as a prophet. In the Hebrew language, the word *prophet* means *inspired*, implying that she was a poet, the Maya Angelou of her day. She was revered, respected, gifted, popular and honored by all. Her presence was always desired, so she was on the *A list* of every hostess. As sister to Moses and Aaron, she received special consideration, but she was very special in her own right. Miriam made every newspaper's top ten list of the most important women year after year.

That's exactly why God had to take her down a peg or two. He had given her more gifts and abilities than any woman had a right to expect. Even though she had one, it's interesting that her husband is never mentioned. She had so much going for her that she didn't need a husband to feel complete. (Neither do you, by the way. You are complete in and of yourself and God himself says he will be your husband (Isaiah 54:5). Single women, read Isaiah 54:1-6 if you are single and wishing you weren't.)

Out of jealousy, Miriam and Aaron began questioning Moses' leadership, because he had married an Ethiopian woman. They spread doubt among the people, trying to undermine Moses' authority. Miriam spoke up, "Is Moses the *only* man God speaks through? I'm a prophet, for goodness' sake! God speaks through *me*, too!" Although that was all true, it wasn't Miriam's place to criticize the leader God had chosen. Moses wasn't perfect by a long shot, but he was God's appointed leader of the entire nation of Israel. He had been called by God — kicking and screaming all the way — to lead Israel to the Promised Land. Miriam and Aaron had been called to assist him. They sort of forgot that little detail. Jealousy and pride made them publicly attempt to put themselves on an equal par with Moses. God had not ordained that Israel be led by a committee of three! (If he had, they would probably still be in Egypt.) He had ordained Moses, imperfect leader that he was, to be the head honcho. Don't think for a moment that Miriam and Aaron didn't know that. They knew it perfectly well, but their pride and jealousy blinded them in their ambition, and God did not tolerate it, squashing the intended coup.

In Numbers 12:4, we're told that God spoke suddenly to Moses, Aaron and Miriam saying, "You three get out here. I want to talk to you." They went. (Wouldn't you?) God came down and stood as a pillar of cloud in the door of the worship tent and commanded only Miriam and Aaron to come closer. Here's the gist of what God said. "I speak to my people through visions and dreams. But I speak to Moses *face to face*. Who are you two to say you're as great as Moses? You've forgotten who he is; you've forgotten who you are; and you've forgotten who I am." Then God's presence left them in a cloud of anger. (I don't know about you, but I don't ever want to hear God talk to me that way!)

The effect of this dressing down on Miriam was immediate and disastrous. She had turned white as snow, and had a terminal case of leprosy — for which there was no vaccine. (Maybe this is where we get the expression *white with fear*.) When you consider the gravity of her situation, it's a wonder she was still breathing! Aaron was petrified, and began babbling and begging forgiveness from his brother, asking him to pray for Miriam's healing. Moses asked God to heal her immediately. But God made them wait awhile. Sin has consequences. He reminded Moses that even a mild punishment from an earthly father would have required her to be by herself outside the camp for a week, so she would have to be in isolation away from everyone she loved for seven days.

This was both a humiliation and a protection for Miriam. She needed time alone to get her heart right with God. If she had been with the people, well-meaning sympathizers and self-appointed righteously indignant Israelites would have given her no time to be alone with God. Sometimes God has to set us aside in order to get through to us. Can you imagine the depth of the soul-searching and bitter remorse she experienced out there all alone? Her only companion was her conscience, and she didn't want to listen to it! It was the worst week of her life. Miriam had been brought as low as she could go. While Miriam was in solitary confinement, *no one* made any progress toward the Promised Land. Because she was in a position of leadership, every Israelite had to cool his or her heels while Miriam got her perspective straightened out. The consequences of one leader's sin affected every single person in the nation. (It isn't much of a quantum leap to draw a modern-day parallel, is it?)

As a child of God, never think for a minute that you can choose to sin and not pay the price. God's chastisement is his mark of ownership on you. If you were not his child, he would let you get away with anything and everything you could dream up. Ever wonder why evil people seem to get away with murder (literally)? It's because they have chosen to ignore God. Yes, there is hope even for the worst of them, and we should pray for them to turn to God, but that is a choice they must make. God has given us all the power to choose whom we will serve — good or evil, God or Satan. Joshua 24:15 says, "Choose you this day whom you will serve."

God gives us a choice. Make sure you make the right one. Decision determines destiny.

Rahab
The Broad From Jericho

God had a purpose in bringing the Israelites out of Egypt. He brought them *out* in order to bring them *in* — to the Promised Land. (Deuteronomy 4:37,38) But it took awhile to work the worldliness of Egypt out of them. Before they could inherit the promises of God and the land he had promised them, he had to wait for the murmuring and complaining, fickle half-hearted-obedience-prone generation to die out. Not one person over the age of twenty who left Egypt under Moses was allowed to enter the Promised Land. Moses taught the new generation the Ten Commandments. (Please note that God did not call them the Ten Suggestions.)

As people of God, we must be people of integrity. Some-body else can leave her empty grocery cart any old place in the parking lot. You cannot — if you're going to be a person of integrity and God's representative. (What would Jesus do with that empty grocery cart? Right. He'd put it in the corral so it would be ready for the next person to use it because he's always thinking of the other person, not himself.) No half-hearted obedience. It's all or nothing.

Christians are to be different from the rest of the world, pointing people to God by the way we talk, the way we dress, the standards we uphold in our homes, and the way we behave toward others. Don't think this is not work! Every single Christian is called by God to do one thing: turn people to him. Some days that's easier than others. That's why it's important to establish good habits, so that on the difficult days, we'll automatically do the right thing.

When God was ready to bring the Israelites into the Promised Land, he took Moses up to the top of Mt. Pisgah and let him see the land he had prepared for his people. And then he took Moses to Heaven and appointed Joshua as his successor.

Joshua had been one of the twelve scouts to check out the land of Canaan, and one of the two who came back with a positive go-get-'em attitude. Joshua had the respect and love of this new generation of Israelites to the same extent that Moses had had the respect and love of the old generation who had all died off in the 40 years of wandering in the desert.

Joshua was a military man. Organized. Efficient. All his socks lined up in a neat row in his drawer. His sandals were always spit-polished. He never did anything halfway. Every day, in every way, he did his very best. No matter what the situation. No matter how he felt. Even if he hated doing it. (He must have been a barrel of laughs to live with..Imagine what would happen if you didn't hang the towel just right!)

Why was Joshua so bold and fearless for God? Because God had given him a promise. "Have not I commanded thee? Be strong and of a good courage; be not afraid, neither be thou dismayed: for the Lord thy God is with thee withersoever thou goest." (Joshua 1:9) That was God's part of the deal. Joshua's part of the deal was simple: believe what God had promised and act on it. We tend to make life too complicated. If you want the best life God has planned for you, do what Joshua did: Believe God's promises and act on them. So simple!

Joshua knew that he was supposed to take the city of Jericho. God gave him a plan. He sent two men into Jericho to assess the situation. They ended up staying overnight at the house of a known harlot, Rahab. In the Hebrew language, the word harlot meant the same thing it does today. There's no nice way to say it: Rahab continually had sex with any man who wanted it — for a fee. How she got to this point in her life, we don't know. What we *do* know is that Jericho was an ungodly city and the people there didn't worship the God of Israel. It had thick walls all the way around for protection, thick enough to build a house on top. That's where Rahab lived — on top of the wall that circled the city of Jericho.

Undoubtedly she was well paid for her services by the men who used them. So it's safe to assume she had furnished her house with the most modern of conveniences and the best of everything. She most likely wore designer clothes and the latest fashions. But there had to have been that God-shaped empty place in her life (the one only God can fill), because when Joshua's two spies showed up, she chose to believe in their God. She protected them and turned her own life around. We all have an emptiness in our lives before we accept God. Nothing else and no one else can fill it. And as soon as you turn to God and accept him as your own, he fills that empty space in your heart to overflowing. The overflow is what blesses those around you.

The night Joshua's two spies spent teaching Rahab about God was the night Rahab's life changed forever. Not only was she a different person, not only did she get her act together, she saved the lives of the two spies and her faith earned her a place on God's honor roll (Hebrews 11:31).

The people of Jericho had heard how the Israelites had left Egypt and how God had protected them and miraculously rescued them from the Egyptians who were chasing them. One citizen of Jericho had seen Joshua's two spies enter Rahab's house and told the king of Jericho. The king sent a messenger to Rahab, commanding her to turn the two spies over to him. Rahab had a decision to make, and she put her faith in the God of Israel and made the right choice — not the easy choice. She told the king's messenger that the men had indeed come to see her, but she hadn't known where they were from and that they had left about the time the city gates were shut for the night and didn't know where they had gone. Then she added, "If you hurry, you can catch them."

Actually, she knew exactly where the two spies were. She had piles of flax stalks laid out to dry on her roof in preparation for making linen from the stem fibers. She had hidden the two men under the piles of flax stalks. As soon as the king's men left in hot pursuit on a wild goose chase, Rahab went up on the roof to talk to the spies. She told them that the whole city was afraid of the Israelites, because of what God had done for them. And she confessed her faith in their God and acknowledged him as the one true God. (Joshua 2:11) It was that faith that saved her life, as well as her soul.

Then she negotiated with them for the lives of her entire family. The two spies agreed to protect her parents, her brothers and sisters and all their possessions when the Israelites took over Jericho. (Such a deal I've got for you!) Her family's lives for the lives of the two spies. They agreed, but being the smart business-woman that she was, she asked for a token of their agreement. They gave her a red rope as a token of their agreement and told her to hang it from her window when the Israelites came to take over the city so she and her family would be protected. Then she let them down the outside of the city wall from her window on the red rope they had given her.

When the Israelites came to conquer Jericho, Rahab hung the red rope from her window as they had said, and her life and the lives of her entire family were spared, as they had agreed. Rahab's faith in God saved them from destruction.

Throughout the Bible we are given symbols of important truths to come. These symbols are called types. The color red is a symbol of sacrifice. It points to the sacrifice of Jesus, who shed his red blood to pay for our redemption and give us the gift of eternal life. Our faith in him saves us.

In Hebrews, chapter 11, we have an honor roll of faithful men and women who were saved by faith in God and his plan of redemption. It is an honor to be included on that list. Rahab's name is in verse 31. She was a woman of faith. You can be, too, if you put your life — body, soul and spirit — into the hands of God and trust in the Redeemer he provided for your eternal security. Faith in him will change your life — forever! You have everything to gain and nothing to lose. Don't try to understand it. Just do it! (Then go out and buy something red as a token of your faith in God.)

Deborah
The Judge Judy Of Her Day

After Joshua died and the Israelites had possessed the Promised Land, they were living their dream. God had kept his part of the bargain and had given his chosen people victory after victory. They were no longer wandering in circles all over the wilderness. They had everything they had ever asked for or even dreamed of. As time went on and life got easier, the Israelites got more complacent. They still sat around the living room repeating their favorite stories of how God had rescued them from this situation or from that threat. Their children grew strong and healthy and life was good. Very good.

Throughout history, whenever times were good, people relaxed and complacency crept in. The Israelites were no different than people are today. They had their little everyday problems, and every once in awhile the men would have to go off and thump some enemy over the head, but life moved on in a positive direction.

During this time, there was no exceptional leader such as Moses or Joshua to lead the nation, other than Judah, a military leader (when he *had* to be in order to keep the borders safe). Joshua loved the Lord and obeyed him completely. He never did anything halfway. However, the other tribal leaders of Israel didn't do as good a job. They had all been raised to know their covenant with God, but their complacency lulled them into half-hearted obedience. They didn't really fight their enemies to win. They were satisfied to subdue them temporarily. (Sounds like the six o'clock news, doesn't it?) As their compromising mind-set grew, their standards and morality lessened. Israel was on a downward slide to disaster and they weren't even aware of it.

God had made it perfectly clear that his chosen people were to keep themselves separate and remember who they were and from where they had come. But their incomplete obedience convinced them that it was okay to intermingle with other peoples who did not know the God of Israel, but worshipped idols. The Israelites were a shadow of their former selves, and very few of them were truly living for the Lord and keeping the laws he had given them through Moses. In fact, the Bible says they were so far gone they were worshipping idols right along with the rest of the world. This was the worst thing of all that was wrong with Israel at that time — the one thing God could not and would not tolerate. It was infidelity of the worst kind.

But God, in his love for his people and in his mercy, raised up judges throughout this dark period of Israel's history to call them back to God. These were not judges as we think of them today. In Hebrew, the word *judge* carries with it an extended meaning of *governing*. Not only did these judges govern, litigate and pass sentence, they also reasoned and pleaded with God's wayward people as they ruled. However, the Bible says all their reasoning and pleading was to no avail. The people of Israel were hell-bent on self-destruction and no amount of pleading or reasoning could turn them around as a nation. We're told in Judges 2:20 that "the anger of the Lord was hot against Israel." That was not an enviable position to be in. They were in for a period of intense testing by God.

Like the U.S. Army, God was looking for a few good men — and women. He found them. One was named Deborah. We're told she was married, a poet, and truly inspired by God, being greatly respected for her wisdom. People came to her constantly and repeatedly for help.

There was another judge nearby named Barak, who was a military man. Deborah knew God had told Barak to wage war on one of Israel's enemies, and she reminded him he needed to do what God had commanded. For some reason (which we are not told), Barak refused to go unless Deborah accompanied him. (This was the equivalent of Norman Schwarzkopf refusing to go to battle unless Janet Reno went with him. Can you imagine it?)

Deborah, however, agreed to go — for the good of Israel — but she lost a lot of respect for Barak right then and there.

She told him point blank that he had forfeited any personal honor or glory he might have earned by waging battle for God, and that the Lord would deliver the enemy into the hand of a woman, to Barak's shame. So they set out together. That must have been some journey! Don't you wish you'd been a fly on Deborah's tent flap?

The morning of the great battle arrived. Deborah had been watching the enemy preparing for battle and assembling troops across the valley. Now 900 iron chariots were lined up and ready to charge Barak's 10,000 men, who had zero chariots. And where was Barak? Sleeping in! Deborah had to go wake him up! In her best Judge Judy voice, Deborah told Barak to get up and get moving. Can't you just hear her? *Barak, you dingbat! Get your act together and get out there! You're supposed to be a leader, so lead!*

That was all Barak needed to hear. He fought brilliantly and led his 10,000 troops to victory. It was such a victory that the enemy general, named Sisera, jumped down from his iron chariot and ran away on foot, deserting his men in the face of the avenging Israelites. Barak and his army killed every single man in Sisera's army, except one — Sisera himself. Why on earth Barak let him get away is beyond imagining. Sisera ran straight to the tent of Jael, the wife of one of his allies. Jael saw Sisera coming as fast as he could run — and all alone — and told him to not be afraid, she would take care of him.

The Bible always tells it like it is, and God minced no words in describing Sisera's complete capitulation to fear. When Jael got him inside, she gave him a drink of milk and put him down for a nap, even tucking him in. (Really! Read it for yourself in Judges 4:18-20.) Just before the mighty military man dozed off, he asked her to stand in the tent door and not tell anyone he was there. Jael was married to a descendant of Moses' father-in-law whose name was Heber (from which the word Hebrew comes). So Jael most likely knew the history of the Israelites, and also knew Israel's God. It's a reasonable explanation of what happened next. While Sisera was in an exhausted deep sleep, Jael nailed him. Literally. She took a long tent-nail (a ten to twelve inch spike) and a hammer and drove it through his head from temple to temple, right into the ground. Sisera never knew what hit him.

Not long after that, Jael spotted Barak pursuing Sisera. She went out and flagged him down, and told him she'd show him the man he was looking for. Can you imagine Barak's chagrin when he saw Sisera lying dead and realized Jael had finished the job for him?

Then Deborah and Barak led Israel in a great celebration, complete with a song of praise from the poet laureate, Deborah, praising God for Israel's victory and giving credit where credit was due — to Jael. Deborah's prophecy to Barak had come true: the enemy had been defeated by the hand of a woman. Because God used two women, Deborah and Jael, Israel had complete victory over its enemy. And then there was peace in Israel for forty years.

The Bible says that during the time of the judges *every man did what was right in his own eyes.* If someone wanted to steal, he just did it. Morality slowed to a crawl. Children were not raised; they were allowed to grow up. The law of the land was not the law of God; it was the law of *if it feels good, do it.*

It's been said that the hand that rocks the cradle rules the world. Deborah was a wife and a mother. She was an ordinary extraordinary woman, because her faith was strong at a time when Israel as a nation had all but forsaken its faith and was not living by the laws God had given them. She was God's woman when God had very few men he could count on. Just so, God has his women throughout the world today. You, too, can be a woman God uses to change the world. All you have to do is give him permission to use you. And then, keep yourself focused on him. He'll do the rest.

Ruth
One Enchanted Evening

Everyone likes a good tear-jerking love story, and God is no exception. Ruth lived in a country named Moab (MOE-ab), populated by the descendants of Abraham's nephew, Lot. Back in Canaan (the Promised Land), there was a famine. One Canaanite, Elimelech (ee-LIMM-eh-leck), took his wife, Naomi, and his two sons, Mahlon (MAY-lawn) and Chilion (KILL-ee-on), and went in search of food. He found what he was looking for in Moab. And then he died.

The literal meaning of peoples' names in the Bible is fascinating. Elimelech literally means *my God is King*. Naomi means *pleasant*. This couple, if they lived up to their names, probably had a very happy life together. He loved God and put him first in every decision. She also loved God, was pleasant to be around, and enjoyed being his wife. Their sons, if they lived up to their names, must have been a different story altogether. Mahlon means *sick* and Chilion means *pining*. Life with those two must have been fun! Somehow, *sick* and *pining* managed to find two women in Moab who could stand them, and they married. One wife was named Orpah (ORE-pah) (*no, not Oprah!*), which meant *deer or fawn*, and one married Ruth, which meant *friendship or beauty*. For about ten years, life for this little family was normal, and then the bottom fell out. Mahlon and Chilion both died. Then there were three widows.

One day down at the local laundromat, Naomi heard that the famine was over back home in Canaan. Without her husband and her two sons, she was in a difficult situation. She couldn't just go out and get a job. Women didn't do that in those days. Naomi felt it was time to go home to Canaan where her relatives could provide for her needs and comfort her in her grief. There was a very strong bond and a deep love among these three women and both Ruth and Orpah decided to move with Naomi to her homeland. They hadn't gone very far on their journey when Naomi suggested they each leave her and go back to their mothers' homes. They didn't want to do that, however, and amid hugs and tears, they both insisted on staying with her.

Naomi was a very logical and sensible woman. She reasoned with them that she was old and wasn't going to have more sons for them to marry. "Even if I got a husband tonight," she argued, "and I gave birth to more sons, would you wait twenty years to marry them? Be sensible, girls! I already feel bad enough that you've lost your husbands and I cannot provide for you. Your whole lives are ahead of you. Go home to your families where you can be taken care of." Then they all burst into tears again.

After they'd gone through the second box of Kleenex, Orpah kissed Naomi goodbye and left. She hadn't gone more than a few feet when she realized she was walking alone. She turned around and saw her sister-in-law, Ruth, still clinging to Naomi. Orpah was torn between love for the family she was with and the fear and uncertainty of moving to a land she had never seen. Orpah did not have the same strength of character or level of commitment to Naomi that Ruth had. So she left. Alone. When the going got tough, she got going — back the way she had come.

Naomi was still reasoning with Ruth, trying to get her to do what she felt was best for her, even if it cost her Ruth's loving companionship. True love puts the other person's needs first, and that's what both Ruth and Naomi were doing. Each of them was insisting on putting the other one first, no matter what it would cost them personally. Ruth made such a heart-wrenching declaration of her love for her mother-in-law that it has become one of the best-loved passages of Scripture and is often used as a wedding vow. "Entreat me not to leave thee, or to return from following after thee: for whither thou goest, I will go; and where thou lodgest, I will lodge: thy people shall be my people, and thy God, my God. Where thou diest, will I die, and there will I be buried. The Lord do so to me, and more also, if ought [anything] but death part thee and me."

(Ruth 1:16 and 17) Beautiful, isn't it? But look beyond the words and analyze what she was really saying here.

One of the strong arguments Naomi had used in trying to persuade Ruth to go with her sister-in-law was that Orpah had gone "back to her people and her gods." From this, it's safe to assume that Orpah had lived in Naomi's Jewish family but had never truly had a relationship with Naomi's God. Ruth, however, declared not only her love for Naomi, but steadfastly declared her commitment to the God of Israel. She cut all ties to her old life and stepped out in faith, trusting Jehovah to take care of her and guide her. By now, the angels must have been using their wings to brush away their tears of joy at such devotion! And God's heart must have been bursting with happiness. How could he *not* be touched at Ruth's declaration of love?

In the face of such love and commitment, Naomi gave up and graciously accepted Ruth's decision. Together, they completed the journey and arrived at Bethlehem, the town Naomi's husband had come from. Naomi was finally home. Her journey was nearly over. But for Ruth, the adventure of her lifetime was just beginning.

Everyone welcomed the two women, but it was a very busy time of year, because they had arrived just as the barley crop was being harvested. Now, social security hadn't yet been invented, but there was a welfare system of sorts. People who needed a helping hand were allowed to walk the fields, gleaning what grain was left behind after the reapers finished. Generous farmers often deliberately left something behind for the *gleaners*, as they were called. Remember that Ruth didn't know one field from the other. The field of corn she just happened to stumble upon belonged to a wealthy farmer named Boaz (BOH-az), who just happened to be a relative of Naomi's by marriage.

Ruth was busy gathering corn for herself and Naomi, and didn't notice the handsome stranger talking with the crew supervisor and watching her every move. She didn't hear him ask who she was. She didn't see the gleam that entered his eye when he was told she was Naomi's widowed daughter-in-law. She just kept picking up corn, and stacking up a large pile in one corner of the storehouse. She had been working since early morning and by the time Boaz got there, it was nearly dinnertime, so she was tired, hot and dirty. Her face, hands and feet were smudged with the good dark earth of

Canaan's soil and the sweat was turning it into muddy little streaks down her flushed cheeks. Her hair was hanging down in sweaty clumps and she hadn't bothered with her make-up that morning, knowing she wouldn't be meeting anyone important that day. (Ever had that happen to you?) To top it all off, she was wearing her oldest and most patched outfit – at least ten years old. (What else would you wear to work in the fields all day?)

On one of her last trips to the storehouse, she sat down to catch her breath. She wasn't used to having to work for her daily bread, and every muscle in her body was screaming for relief. As she put her head back against the wall and closed her eyes, she couldn't believe she had taken her last two aspirin only an hour ago!

Enter Boaz. Freshly showered, wearing the latest Guccis and smelling of English Leather aftershave, this disgustingly rich, gorgeous hunk approached her and quietly spoke her name. Startled, she listened to his offer of provision and protection. She couldn't believe her ears, and asked him why he was being so good to her. Then he told her he knew who she was and how she had stayed with Naomi through all that had happened to them. He told her God would reward her hard work because she had put her faith and trust in him (Ruth 2:12). And then he invited her to stay for dinner. What do you think her first thought was? Right! Of all the days to *not* wear make-up! Talk about a work ethic! I would have run home to get cleaned up. Not Ruth. She went back to the field in a happy daze and finished up the day's work, gleaning all the grain she could. At dinner, she sat with the reapers at Boaz' table and he himself passed her the food. At the end of the meal, she went home and fell into bed exhausted.

The next morning, Ruth went to the farm of Boaz to glean again. She didn't know that Boaz had instructed his reapers to let her glean wherever she wanted, and to accidentally let some handfuls of grain fall into her path on purpose. Have you ever had *handfuls of purpose* fall into your life? Unexpected blessings that warmed your heart and delighted your soul? That was God's taking care of you, just as Boaz quietly took care of Ruth. It might have been an unexpected check in the mail, or a call from an old friend you hadn't talked to in ages. Little surprises sent by God on purpose, just to show his love for you. Because of the handfuls of purpose Boaz instructed his men to leave for Ruth, at the end of the second day, she had over a bushel of barley. When Naomi saw how well she had done, she knew something unusual had happened, and she asked her where she had gleaned that day. When Naomi heard it was the farm of someone named Boaz, she said a prayer of thanks in her heart and explained to Ruth that Boaz just happened to be a close relative, from Elimelech's side of the family.

That didn't mean much to Ruth until Naomi explained some of the finer points of Jewish law to her. The law provided a solution to the widows' problem. It was a far different culture that Ruth lived in than a young widow lives in today. There was no life insurance from her husband, no IRA or stock portfolio. Ruth had next to nothing, because Naomi also had nothing. There was a provision in the law that a man who was a close relative of the widow could redeem her inheritance by purchasing the deceased husband's estate, but it had to be done with the sanction of the city council. That would clear the way for Boaz to marry Naomi and make sure she received her late husband's estate. (You have to remember that in those days women didn't automatically inherit; the men had all the rights.) This was the only way Ruth could be protected and cared for: Boaz would have to buy Naomi's estate and care for her so he could also care for Ruth.

Boaz knew the law, and he knew his duty to his widowed relatives. He called a meeting of the city council, invited the only other male relative who could possibly have redeemed Naomi's inheritance for her, and presented his case. And then he held his breath. Would the other man do what was necessary and end up with Ruth? (What a plot! Danielle Steel couldn't have done better!) The other kinsman said that yes, he would redeem Naomi's inheritance.

Then Boaz played his trump card. He doubled the cost of the land (the inheritance) by insisting that the other kinsman also buy Ruth's husband's portion of the land he would have inherited as Elimelech's son and heir. That was more than the other relative could handle, and he backed down. He couldn't pay the price. Boaz won. He sealed the deal by taking off his shoe and giving it to the man beside him as earnest money. (There were also some very funny points of Jewish law!) Not only did Boaz do the right thing in the right way, he rescued Naomi and Ruth. At last all was well with the house of Elimelech. Ruth and Boaz married and named their first son Obed (OH-bed), whose grandson was David, Israel's greatest king. And they all lived happily ever after.

Lest you think this is just a lovely little story, let's look a little deeper. Boaz is a wonderful type of Christ, an Old Testament preview of what Christ would be like. Note the comparisons:

Boaz was the only one who was able to redeem Ruth.

Christ is the only one able to redeem mankind.

He helped her when she couldn't help herself.

Due to our sinful nature, we are unable to help ourselves.

He paid the price of her redemption in full.

Christ satisfied the requirements of the law in full, enabling him to purchase our redemption.

He put his money where his mouth was. (It cost him to redeem her.)

Christ paid the ultimate price by sacrificing his life instead of requiring us to sacrifice ours.

He loved her and chose her for his bride.

Christ loved the church (believers) and chose us to be his bride.

He provided for her every need.

There is no need we can have that Christ has not already provided for.

He elevated her to a position of honor.

Christ has made us sons and daughters of Almighty God, giving us the highest honor it is possible for a human being to have.

He used her to bless the world.

Christ has no other plan than to use his children to reach the world and bless those he brings across our paths.

Many, years later, Ruth's grandson, David, became the ancestor of Jesus of Nazareth. Not only did God provide for Ruth, he honored her by placing her in Jesus' family tree. When we place ourselves in his hands, God always does more than we can imagine. Just as he had a wonderful future planned for Ruth, he has a perfect plan for you, too. Don't mess it up by taking matters into your own hands when things aren't going just the way you want them to. Trust him to work things out in his way and in his timing. You want to live happily ever after, too, don't you?

Hannah
Getting Her Heart's Desire By Giving It Up

We don't know much about Hannah, except that her husband loved her greatly and that she felt like a huge failure. You'll remember from the story of Sarah that in the Hebrew culture, it was considered a reproach to be childless. Hannah was one of two women married to Elkanah (ELK-ah-nah), a Jewish man who worshipped God. His other wife, Peninnah (pen-NINE-ah), had children, but Hannah had none. In I Samuel, 1:4, we are told that Elkanah treated Peninnah and her children with respect and provided well for them. When it came time for him to make the annual sacrifice to God, Elkanah made the usual sacrifices for Peninnah and her children, but for Hannah, he made a worthy sacrifice (verse 5), because he loved her, and he ached for her unhappiness at being childless.

Unfortunately, Peninnah knew how to press her advantage, and she made Hannah's life miserable. She flaunted her ability to have children at every opportunity, rubbing salt in Hannah's already gaping wound. As the years went by, it only got worse. It got so bad that Hannah was beside herself with grief and longing. All she wanted was to hold her own child in her arms and smell that sweet baby smell and feel him nursing at her breast. Was that so much to ask?

She was so miserable, she stopped smiling. She couldn't sleep and she couldn't eat. She just cried her way through box after box of Kleenex until Elkanah was worried sick. It was killing him to see her so miserable. "Aren't I better to you than ten sons?" he asked as he held her in his arms, trying to comfort her.

As much as he might want to, how could any man possibly

60

understand the depth of a woman's longing in her soul for her own child? Motherhood is a special blessing God designed just for women. There's absolutely nothing that can fill the emptiness of a woman's heart like giving birth to her own baby. Men — and fathers — have other blessings that God designed just for them, and we women cannot fully appreciate them. That's why it takes *both* a mother and a father to create and raise a child. God planned it that way.

When Hannah had plunged so deeply into despair that she simply could stand it no longer, she went to the temple to pray. It's not that she hadn't been praying, but this time was different. Up until now, Hannah wanted a child because she had none and something was missing in her life. No doubt she had tried all the standard methods of getting pregnant, including taking her temperature to determine when she was ovulating, and all the aphrodisiacs known at that time. (Elkanah probably never wanted to see another oyster as long as he lived!)

When she arrived at the temple, she wept bitterly. This was more than just a crying jag. This was a gut-wrenching, "I-don't-care-who-sees-my-red-blotchy-face" agony of soul pouring out of Hannah. From the depths of her heart and spirit, she cried out to God. But this time, she made a vow. She promised God that if he would give her a son, she would give him back to God to serve him all the days of his life. To make sure God knew she was serious, she promised that his hair would never be cut. This doesn't sound like much of a sacrifice to us, but in those days, when people separated themselves to serve God, not cutting their hair was a sign of their separation or dedication. These dedicated servants of God were known as Nazarites (NAZZ-ah-rights), and they date back to the days of Moses. By this vow, God knew Hannah had finally gone beyond her natural desire to have a baby to bring herself joy and fulfillment. Her vow proved that she was ready to give God the thing that was dearer to her than life itself: her son.

All the time Hannah was praying, her lips were moving, although she made no audible sound. The priest, Eli, had been watching her as he sat on the porch of the temple. When he saw her crying her eyes out and her lips moving, he assumed she was drunk and approached her. "You should be ashamed of yourself," he said to her, "being this drunk so early in the morning. You must stop drinking!" Startled, she poured out her grief to him and told him her heart's desire. To his credit, Eli immediately believed her and assured her that God would answer her prayer.

Something happened in Hannah when Eli said those words of assurance. Something inside her just clicked into place, and an inexplicable peace settled over her. She knew — she just knew in her heart that she was going to have a son. She had such peace in her soul that she stopped on her way home to get something to eat and peace settled over her face. Her husband took one look at her and knew she was going to be fine. The next day, after returning from the worship service at the temple, Hannah and Elkanah's son was conceived in joy.

What an exciting, deliriously happy time the next nine months must have been! (For one thing, Peninnah was probably noticeably quiet around the house.) The expectant father converted his home office into a nursery, while the expectant mother devoured every baby book she could get her hands on and looked up Dr. Spock on the Internet. Life became a round of Lamaze classes, piles of diapers, and baby blankets in every shade of blue imaginable. No baby was ever wanted more than the one Hannah carried in her womb and in her heart.

When their son finally arrived, Hannah named him Samuel, which means *asked of God*, because she had, indeed, asked God for him. In the midst of her joy, Hannah did not forget her promise to God. She knew that Samuel would be hers for only a short time, and then he would leave her to serve God. He was God's and had only been loaned to her with the awesome responsibility of giving little Samuel the right start in life.

How vital are those first few years in a child's life! Babies are so helpless and so needy! It's a huge responsibility to be a parent. Sometimes you can do absolutely every single thing exactly right, and the kid still gets into trouble. At those times, all a parent can do is give the child to God, because sometimes he is the only one who can get the kid's attention and straighten him or her out. That's when the parent has to remember that the child is just on loan, and really belongs to God. All you can do is continually give your children back to God, minute by minute. You may have to take your hands off your child's future and let God direct it. It may tear you apart to let go, but if you don't, you may get in the way of what God is trying to do.

Every child has a will, and there will come a day when he or she will have to answer for his or her own actions and reactions. You cannot live your child's life. You can only live your own. (That's usually enough to keep anyone busy.)

Hannah was the consummate mother. She gave her son to God before he was even a gleam in her husband's eye. She loved him more than she loved her own life. She raised him well, and taught him what he needed to know in order to become a man of God. She nursed him when he was sick, fed him when he was hungry, put a coin under his pillow when he lost his baby teeth, comforted him when he was frightened, and taught him to put God first in his life. And when she finally weaned him, she took him to Eli, the priest, and gave him her only son to minister for the Lord for the rest of his life. She kept her promise to God, as hard as that was for her to do. And God honored her faithfulness with five more children, three sons and two daughters.

A mother's love never dies. Every year Hannah made Samuel a little coat and took it to him when the family went to make the annual sacrifice at the temple. Samuel grew up to be a wise and respected man of God, loved both by God and the people he ministered to. He had a profound influence on the entire nation of Israel — all because of a woman's broken heart and her faithfulness to God. Never underestimate the power of a mother's influence on her children, nor the willingness of God to give you the deepest desires of your heart.

Esther
Queen Of Hearts

The little book of Esther does not mention God even once, but nowhere in the Scriptures is God more conspicuous than he is in this short story of a beautiful young Jewish woman who put her life on the line to save the lives of the Jews living in captivity in Persia.

At the time of Esther, the Israelites had survived many years of wars, but they had survived in little scattered groups, living in captivity. As a people, they had not kept God's law and had worshipped other gods — the one thing God refused to tolerate. There were a few who still honored the God of Abraham, but they were definitely the minority.

One of these surviving remnants of Israelites was in Persia. When the reigning queen of Persia, Vashti (VASH-tee), openly disobeyed the king's command, the government officials were afraid all the women in the land would follow her example and a feminist movement would take hold, fostering a wave of contempt and anger directed at the men's authority. (Word for word, that's what they said! Check out Esther 1:17 and 18. Who said the Bible had no relevance in today's world? When American women began insisting on their rights, American men gave *the exact same arguments*!)

The king's advisors recommended that Queen Vashti be deposed and divested of her estate and that another woman be made queen in her place. "Then all the wives in the country will honor their husbands," they reasoned. What foolishness! As if respect could be legislated! (The entire country had just finished a rip-roaring national celebration that lasted 180 days, so they probably weren't thinking straight at the time!)

The king liked the idea, however, and that was the end of Vashti. He sent letters to all 127 of his provinces (each written in the province's own language), making it a law that "every man was the ruler in his own house." (That's a direct quote!) How far do you think that law would get today? If you had to have a law so the women would know the men were in charge, it says a lot about the men, don't you think?

It was from this mess that a beautiful young Jewish woman named Esther (or Hadassah (hah-DASS-ah)) was chosen to be Queen of Persia. Esther's parents were both dead and she had been raised by her older cousin, Mordecai. Not only beautiful, but smart, Esther did as Mordecai had advised her and did not immediately reveal the fact that she was Jewish.

For a whole year, Esther lived in the king's harem with all the other would-be queens, but she was so obviously queen material that she was given seven maids of her own and a special suite of rooms within the harem. Mordecai visited her every day and suggested ways to enhance the chances that she would be the next queen. They needn't have worried. When her turn came to appear before the king, there was no contest. She became his new queen. Through all of this, she did not reveal that she was Jewish, because Mordecai knew that when the time was right, God would use Esther to save the lives of her countrymen.

While Mordecai and Esther were biding their time, things began to happen. Mordecai learned that two of the king's cabinet members were planning on killing the king. He told Esther about the assassination plot and she warned the king, giving Mordecai the credit. Then the king appointed a man named Haman (HAY-men) as his next-in-command, and ordered everyone in the country to bow to Haman and reverence him whenever they saw him. The word *reverence* used here implied *worship*, not mere respect for his office. This presented a real problem to Mordecai, the Jew, because God had forbidden his people to worship any man; they were to worship only him. So Mordecai took a stand as a Jew, and refused to prostrate himself and worship Haman. Day after day, Mordecai stood quietly while everyone else bowed down. Day after day the king's men urged Mordecai to be like everyone else and obey the king's law. But Mordecai answered to a higher law and, although he was courting disaster, he stood tall and straight when Haman was around. By this time, everyone knew that Mordecai was a Jew, and Haman was beside himself with fury. He could not ignore this direct disobedience to the king's law, nor the personal affront to his own pride.

Haman went to the king and proposed a complete annihilation of all the Jews living in Persia. To sweeten the deal, Haman offered to pay the executioners twenty million dollars out of his own pocket, which would be added to the king's treasury. The king didn't have to do a thing, just give Haman permission to eradicate these lawbreakers from the face of the Earth. The king agreed, and told Haman the Jews were his to do with as he saw fit. Then the king issued a written order that every Jew — man, woman and child — in every one of his 127 provinces was to be killed on the thirteenth day of the twelfth month. It was to be done all on the same day, everywhere in the country. The messengers were dispatched with copies of the decree and the king and Haman shared a celebratory drink. (Apparently, ethnic cleansing is nothing new.)

When Mordecai heard the news, he tore his clothes, put on sackcloth and rubbed ashes on his body and stood before the gate to the king's palace, crying at the top of his voice. He wasn't the only one. Many Jews throughout the land did the same thing in their towns. News of her cousin's strange actions reached Esther. She was grief-stricken, and sent some decent clothes to him, but he refused to accept them. She sent her messenger back again and begged him to tell her what was wrong. He not only told her the entire story, he sent her a copy of the king's death warrant for all the Jews and told her it was time for her to go to the king and plead for the lives of her people, him included.

This put Esther in a terrible position. Not only was the king unaware that Esther was a Jew herself, he had not invited her to see him for the past thirty days. Mordecai was asking her to literally put her life on the line for her people and her God. If she went to the king uninvited, she was almost certainly going to be killed, unless he agreed to see her. Esther sent the message back to her cousin that it was suicide for her to go unbidden to the king. Did he realize what he was asking her to risk? His reply was blunt. "This death warrant has your name on it, too, my daughter. You are also a Jew. If you keep your secret and refuse to take a stand with your people and your God, our deliverance will come from somewhere else, and you will be destroyed anyway. It may well be that God has elevated you to be queen in order that you might be his instrument in saving the lives of thousands of his chosen people. *Your* people, Esther."

That moved Esther to action. She knew what she had to do and she determined to do it. She sent word to Mordecai asking him to gather all the Jews in the city together and have them all fast for her, and she would do the same with her court maidens as well. After the three days of fasting, she would go to the king (in direct disobedience to his law) and if she died for doing the right thing, so be it. Her exact words were, "If I perish, I perish."

Mordecai did as she asked and at the end of the third day, Esther dressed in her royal robes and went and stood where the king would see her. How her maids must have tried to dissuade her from risking her life for people she didn't even know! How brave Esther was! God gave her not only the courage to do the right thing, he also gave her a plan to turn the tables on Haman.

When the king saw Esther standing quietly in the wings of the throne room, he invited her to approach him and asked her what she wanted. Whatever it was, he'd give it to her, even if it were half of his kingdom. (That man must have really loved her!) Esther wisely asked for only one thing: that both the king and Haman come to a banquet, which she would host in their honor the next day.

Smart woman. Who could refuse an invitation like that? If the king was pleased by her invitation, Haman was overjoyed. He was so full of himself and so in awe of his own importance that the queen would honor him this way, that he went home and boasted to all his friends and family. To hear him tell it, there was no place for his career and prestige to go except straight up. (Wouldn't you just love to stick a pin in that big, fat ego of his? Esther did even better than that.)

As far as Haman was concerned, there was only one little fly in the ointment of his glorious future, and his name was

Mordecai. It drove him nuts to see that troublesome Jew standing straight and tall in his sackcloth and ashes when everyone else bowed down before Haman. His wife suggested a solution: build a gallows about eight feet high and ask the king to hang Mordecai on it the next day, so there would be nothing to spoil his total enjoyment at the banquet with the king and queen. (Brilliant. That's the spirit: if there's something that's bugging you, squash it. Don't bother considering that you might be able to learn something from it.) This suggestion appealed immensely to Haman. He would finally be free of Mordecai and everything would be just the way he wanted it. Immediately, he ordered the gallows built.

That night, Haman slept like a baby. The king, on the other hand, couldn't get to dreamland no matter what he tried. So he woke one of his servants up and asked for the history book of his own reign to be read to him. When the reader got to the part about Mordecai saving the king's life by warning him about the two cabinet members who had planned to assassinate him, the king asked what honor and dignity had been bestowed upon Mordecai for his loyalty. The answer was *nothing*. By that time, it was the wee hours of the morning and Haman was already standing in the outer court of the king's chamber, waiting to speak to him about hanging the Jew, Mordecai. When the king discovered that Mordecai had gone unrewarded for his faithfulness, he decided that Haman, was exactly the right person to do the honors, and he told his servants to bring him in.

In he came, full of pomposity and self-importance. The king asked him with a smile, "What shall be done to the man whom the king delights to honor." Haman was so far beyond simple pride at this point that it would never have occurred to him that the king was referring to someone else and he immediately thought, "To whom would the king delight to do honor more than to myself?" (Esther 6:6) He reasoned, *If I'm going to be honored by the queen tonight and by the king today, I have arrived! I'd better think BIG!* So Haman suggested a fitting tribute to such a loyal subject would be the king's hand-me-down royal robes, his horse, and the royal crown that he wore on his head. To top it all off, he thought it would be the highest honor possible to have one of the most noble princes of the realm take the robes, horse, and crown to the honoree and put it on him. Then the one being honored should be led on the king's horse through the city streets while the one leading the horse proclaimed, "This is what is done to the man whom the king delights to honor." Since the honor was surely for himself, Haman spared no expense in planning it.

Apparently, the idea pleased the king. He decided it would be a fitting tribute to the man who had been so faithful and loyal to him, and he knew just the right person to deliver the honor. As a huge smile split Haman's face ear to ear, the king commanded Haman to do everything he had proposed to Mordecai, the Jew who sat at the gate to the palace. And before Haman's grin could slide off his face, he warned him to not omit one tiny detail in honoring Mordecai. (Way to go, King!! You finally woke up!)

Haman had no choice; he did exactly as he had proposed for himself, but he did it for Mordecai. After he delivered Mordecai to the king's gate, arrayed in all his royal robes and sitting on the king's own horse, wearing the royal crown upon his Jewish head, there was nothing for Haman to do but cover his head and slink home through the back streets and alleys in mourning for the death of his ambitions and dreams. His wife and his friends couldn't believe their eyes when Haman sneaked into his house and barred the door behind him. This was supposed to be the greatest day of his life! Wasn't this the night the queen herself was going to honor him with a banquet? When Haman told them what had happened, they warned him that since the king had chosen to exalt Mordecai — a Jew who was scheduled to die on the thirteenth with every other Jew in the land — Haman's future was in jeopardy. And, by the way, hadn't that Jewish massacre been Haman's idea in the first place? While they were still talking about Haman's unbelievable reversal of fortune, the king's chamberlains arrived to escort him to the queen's banquet.

By now, Haman was wallowing in denial and feeling slightly better about his future. Surely nothing bad could happen to him if the queen was honoring him. Ignoring the little warning blips flitting across the screen of his mind, he walked proudly beside the king into Queen Esther's banquet. You have to realize that this was a country and a royal couple who really knew how to celebrate in style. The banquet was not a one-evening event. It lasted for days and days — a festival. How Esther kept up appearances through the first twenty-four hours is amazing. She never let on what was on her mind. Neither the king nor Haman had any inkling there was anything amiss. Haman began to relax and enjoy himself. On the second day of the festival, which poor little Haman thought was still to honor him, the king once again asked Esther what request she wanted him to grant her. Whatever it was, all she had to do was state it, and it would be done. Esther looked around her at the lush surroundings, the exquisite beauty of the royal furnishings and the platters of exotic food and the best the king's wine cellar had to offer and knew the moment had come.

Her request was stated plainly and simply: "Let me and my people live. If we had been sold into slavery, I would have held my tongue, but we are to be destroyed," she said. Her request was for the lives of her people, the Jews. This was the first moment that the king knew Esther was a Jew. The entire roomful of people held their breath as Esther waited for the king to answer. When he finally found his voice, his love for Esther triumphed over everything else and, remembering the death warrant he had signed for all the Jews, his anger was hot and quick. He didn't want to lose Esther! If his decree were to be carried out, she would have to die along with her people. The king demanded that Esther tell him who had dared to presume in his heart to put the king into this position. The air was crackling with suspense as slowly and regally, Esther locked her eyes with the king's and told him, "The adversary and enemy is this wicked Haman." In the shocked silence that followed, all the color drained from Haman's face and his legs gave out from under him. The king was so completely angry he stormed from the room and into the garden. Haman marshaled his failed strength one last time and stood up to request mercy from Queen Esther. He knew she was his only hope of surviving the king's wrath.

In order to understand the setting for this drama, we must remember that when a banquet of this magnitude and importance was held, it was not unusual to have couches (or *beds*, as they were called) in the room for the guests to recline upon. The king was still in the garden, and Queen Esther had gone to rest on one of the gold couches. On shaky legs, Haman made his way to Esther. He was probably trying to kneel at her bedside to beg for his life, but this was the wine-tasting day of the banquet, and undoubtedly Haman had sampled every one of the vintages available. In his fear, instead of kneeling at her beside, he lost his balance and fell upon the bed where Esther could only look at him, revolted. With the precise timing of a Hollywood cliffhanger, the king chose this very moment to return from the garden. He could not believe his eyes! He exploded, "Will he also force the queen before me in the house?" Haman thought things could not get any worse, but he was wrong. His time had run out.

At a signal from the king, his men covered Haman's face and prepared to remove him from the room in disgrace. Then one of the chamberlains told the king that the gallows Haman had built to hang Mordecai was completed and was standing at Haman's house. Acknowledging Haman's total betrayal, the king issued a terse command: "Hang *him* on it." And they did.

The king gave all Haman's possessions to Queen Esther, and she then told him that Mordecai was her cousin who had raised her when her parents died. The king had Mordecai brought before him and his court. Can you imagine Esther's joy as she watched the king take the ring off his own finger and place it on Mordecai's hand? (This was the same ring he had given to Haman earlier and had taken back when Haman was hanged.) Then in complete accord with God's idea of justice, Esther made Mordecai the head of Haman's former estate. And then, in regal, dignified humbleness of spirit, she asked the king to reverse the death warrant on the Jews living in his kingdom.

The king not only granted her request, he told Esther and Mordecai to draft the new edict themselves, however they wanted to word it, and to seal it with his ring. This assured that the decree preserving the Jews was final and irreversible. Mordecai was exalted, Esther reigned beside her king with grace and wisdom, and all the enemies of the Jews within the king's

71

domain — from India to Ethiopia — were destroyed at Esther's request. In marvelous understatement, chapter 8 verse 17 says, "...the Jews had joy and gladness, a feast and a good day."

It had been a good day, indeed, when Esther had come into the Persian kingdom. God's people were saved from destruction once again, because a brave and wise woman took a stand for what she knew was right, even if it meant certain death for herself. God's justice always triumphs if we do things his way and wait for him to zap those who work against him. He zaps better than anyone!

You may think you are just an ordinary person, with no particular claim to fame, and you may think God could never use you to change anyone's life, much less change the world. The fact is, if you are living your life for God, you may never know in this lifetime how God has used you to bless others. The simple truth is that God doesn't always use the wise people of the world, the wealthy, or those in positions of authority to give him a physical presence in the world. He doesn't need our abilities, you see. He just needs our availability. All God wants from each of us is our willingness to be a simple conduit through which he can flow.

The Silent Years

Between the end of the Old Testament and the beginning of the New Testament, there was a period of 400 years in the history of Israel. It was a difficult time, filled with division, civil unrest, wars, exile and a growing desperation for the long-anticipated Messiah. (When he finally *did* arrive, most didn't recognize him.) Forty years before Jesus was born, Herod was appointed king of the Jews by the Roman government. This was the same man who reigned when Jesus was born in Bethlehem.

We do not have a written record of God's dealings with the Jews during that time. It's not that God was silent for 400 years. He didn't go away somewhere and pout because people weren't living up to his standards. During every period of human history, God has spoken to and through individuals who believed in him and trusted his promise of a Messiah. We just don't have a record of what he said and did during that time. (That's on my personal list of questions to ask when I finally sit down in Heaven.)

Technically, the four Gospels (Matthew, Mark, Luke and John) are part of the *Old* Testament, not the New Testament. Jesus was born a Jew, under the old covenant God had established with Abraham a couple of thousand years before. The new *covenant* (another word for *testament*) didn't go into effect until *after* Jesus' resurrection. Jesus was an Old Testament Jew, and he lived his earthly life under the same law that was given to Moses — even though he came in order to fulfill the requirements of that law. His sacrificial death was that fulfillment.

The gospel accounts of the events in Jesus' earthly life were never intended to be a complete biography. There is much we do not know. But everything we *do* need to know is there: his eternal existence, human lineage, birth, ministry, teachings, death resurrection and ascension. Why didn't God see fit to include the rest of the details? We can only assume it's because we didn't need to know those things in order to know Jesus. Taken together and synthesized into one composite, chronological whole (called *The Synoptic Gospels*), we do have a portrait of Jesus, the Christ, the Son of God, and the Son of Man — at one and the same time both human and divine.

The writers of the four Gospels wrote down what they saw and heard as they traveled with Jesus during his three-year ministry. Each writer — Matthew, the law-abiding tax collector; Mark, the Generation X representative of his day; Luke, the esteemed doctor; John, the career fisherman — each gave his Gospel account the flavor of his own personality. Although none of the four writers described what he himself thought of Jesus, each Gospel emphasizes a different aspect of Jesus' character. Matthew puts emphasis on the kingship of Jesus; Mark portrays his servant attitude; Luke reveals his humanity and healing power; John reverberates with his divinity. And that doesn't even begin to cover it all! It's safe to say that no matter how many times you read any of the Gospels, if you read with an open mind, a tender heart, and an eager spirit, you'll learn something about God that you didn't notice before. Unfortunately (or maybe fortunately), we can never learn it all. So we need to apply everything we *do* learn about him.

It's interesting to note that nowhere in the Gospels does anyone describe what Jesus looked like. Was he tall, short, dark, pale, handsome, not so handsome? Personally, I don't really care what he looked like. It's much more important to focus on his character and what he taught. Don't get hung up on details that don't matter. What matters — both now and for eternity — is that you believe in him. John 21:25 says, "And there are also many other things which Jesus did, the which, if they should be written every one, I suppose that even the world itself could not contain the books that should be written. Amen." That goes for the Internet, too. What we don't know about Jesus is greater than all of cyberspace. So let's concentrate on what we *do* know, and let's do it by continuing to follow *his-story* through the lives of the women in the New Testament.

At the time Jesus was born, Judea (the northern part of Israel) was under the rule of the Roman Empire, and that made life very difficult for the Jews. Extremely disciplined, never without their weapons, ready for any disciplinary action they felt was necessary, the omnipresent Roman soldiers practiced every day what the contemporary historian, Josephus, called unbloody battles, preparing for the real thing should the need arise. They were ready for anything at a moment's notice. You can imagine the tension and resentment in Jewish towns when the Roman army made itself at home on Jewish turf. To further disturb the town, it was the army's practice to give a trumpet blast whenever they changed activities (even when they were about to go to sleep), so these raucous reminders of their presence loudly inserted themselves throughout the day and night. No wonder they were unwanted guests!

It wasn't easy to be a Roman soldier. The motivation for their extreme discipline was fear. Any infraction of the rules or the least little appearance of laziness or inactivity could result in capital punishment. It was impossible for a Roman soldier to take his position lightly, and just as impossible for the Jews to carry on a normal lifestyle when every time they turned around, they bumped smack into the Roman Empire — an unwelcome intrusion in their home.

The Romans took over every aspect of daily life for the Jews, even intruding into their places of worship and insinuating themselves in ways that were abhorrent to the Jews. For example, any carved image used for worship was the worst kind of offense to the spiritual values of the Jews, being in direct violation of the second commandment of Mosaic Law (Exodus 20:4). The Romans not only had dozens of carved images for all their gods and goddesses, they also worshipped Caesar, their emperor, and carried the carved representations of him on their uniforms, coins and weapons. Because of this, any Roman presence in Jewish places of worship was a direct slap in the face of the all-powerful Jewish religious leaders and (in their eyes), a particularly abhorrent sin. It is little wonder that the Jews hated the Romans with a vengeance. The Jews began to see the promised Messiah as an answer to their Roman problem. It was understandable that the Jews had grown complacent, waiting for his appearance for thousands of years. Their understanding of the Messiah's mission shifted from a spiritual salvation to a physical one. They wanted the hideous Roman Empire out of their lives and their homeland! Why wasn't God sending their Messiah to help them?

Into this political and spiritual powder keg, to a normal, unpretentious family, a baby was born — Jesus, the first son of

Mary of Nazareth. You'll notice I did not say the first son of Mary and Joseph. That's because, even though Joseph was Mary's husband, he was not the biological father of Jesus. *No* human being was the father of Jesus. The Bible is very clear about that fact, and we'll discuss it in more depth in the chapter on Mary of Nazareth. The Messiah's conception by the Holy Spirit and birth through a young virgin, along with his atoning, sacrificial death, and his bodily resurrection from the dead are the pillars that support Christianity.

Without getting into a lot of theology here, consider the humble egg. It has three parts: shell, white, and yolk. Without any one of those three elements, you don't have the whole egg. Just so, without the virgin birth of Jesus, or without the shedding of his innocent blood as payment for every sin ever committed, or without his victorious and bodily resurrection from the dead, or without the coming of the Holy Spirit — you don't have complete Christianity. You only have a nice little philosophy to live by. The *power* is missing.

Women were the first to believe in Jesus as the Messiah. Women ministered to him, taking care of his physical and human emotional needs. Many would say that women are not treated equally in this world, and they would be right. In the 21 century it is still true that women get paid less to do the same work as men. It is still true that women are violently abused by the very people who have promised to love them and care for them. But that is the result of man's inhumanity to man. It was never God's plan. God liberated women in the Garden of Eden when he promised Eve that a woman would be the means he would use to give himself a physical presence in the world. Sixty generations later, Mary of Nazareth was chosen by God to give birth to his son, Jesus. It was the single most important pivotal point in history. Without a woman, it wouldn't have happened. Yes, I know. Without a woman named Eve, it wouldn't have *needed* to happen! But it did, so let's talk about Mary, the teenager who got pregnant out of wedlock — with no help from any man.

Mary
The Unmarried Pregnant Teenager

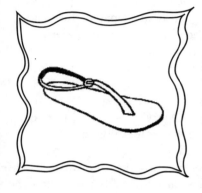

How many times have you heard it? *She's fourteen and pregnant ... disgraceful! Her parents are so embarrassed, I don't know how they're going to handle it.* Teenage pregnancy in the 21 century is nothing new. In fact, it's become so commonplace in our society that we simply tally the statistics and often don't give the individuals involved a second thought. But Mary of Nazareth was not just an ordinary teenager; she was also extraordinary. Mary was every parent's dream: loving, honest, sincere, thoughtful, and totally sold out to God. That doesn't mean she was abnormal, or so heavenly-minded she was no earthly good. But she was unusual, even for the time in which she lived.

It was the custom in Mary's day for girls to marry young. It is generally accepted by Bible scholars that Mary of Nazareth was around fourteen years old when she and Joseph became engaged. The Greek word *espoused* used in Matthew 1:18 means *betrothed* or *engaged*, and implies that an engagement gift, such as a ring, has been given to the woman as a symbol of the engagement. In those days, being engaged was almost as good as being married. Almost. But not quite. There was no sex before the wedding. The highest priority was placed on the young woman's virginity. In fact, stoning was the penalty for a woman's being sexually unfaithful during her betrothal period. It was serious stuff. The Greek word for *virgin* literally means *unknown*, as in never having had intercourse. Mary was every man's dream wife — spiritually, emotionally, intellectually, and physically. What a catch!

Every parent has dreams for his or her children, and Mary's parents were no different. By the time we meet Mary in the

Bible, she was already engaged to Joseph. Her days were filled with preparations for the wedding, wonderful times with her beloved husband-to-be, and dreams of the family they would raise in their long life together. Stars in her eyes, she planned her wedding day, revised the guest list, helped her mother plan the food for the wedding feast, and nervously anticipated the first time she and Joseph would sleep together. It was a wonderful time for Mary, and she lived every moment to the fullest. Everything was proceeding according to plan. And then, in a split second, everything changed — forever.

One day as Mary was trying on her wedding dress for the umpteenth time, a man showed up at Mary's door. To Mary, he looked like a normal man, but there was something about him that made her stop all movement and all thought and listen to him. She became very still, her eyes meeting his. She was not afraid, just expectant. She was a few days away from marrying the man of her dreams; how could anything go wrong? Mary's visitor was not a man, however, but the angel Gabriel, sent specifically by God to give her the news of her life. What Gabriel told her not only changed her life, but the life of every person who has lived since that moment in time. Lovingly, Gabriel, spoke to her: *Hail, you who are highly favored; the Lord is with you. You are blessed among all women.* Mary wondered what kind of greeting that was. (Not your usual, *Hi, how are you?*) Gabriel told her not to be afraid and that God was pleased with her. Then he told her she would give birth to the long-awaited Messiah. By quoting the ancient Messianic prophecies of Isaiah and Daniel, Gabriel told her these things in a way that left no doubt in her mind that it was, indeed, the Messiah, he was talking about, the Son of God.

Mary's immediate reaction to Gabriel's astounding announcement was perfectly human. *How can this be, since I've never slept with a man?* A perfectly logical question. What Gabriel was saying was humanly impossible. Tenderly, Gabriel explained that the child would be the Son of God, fathered by the Holy Spirit. He told her to call the baby *Jesus*, and that he would fulfill all the promises God had made to Adam, Abraham, Jacob, Isaac and all the others down through the centuries. Then he made another startling announcement: Mary's elderly cousin, Elisabeth, was six months pregnant — a woman who had been unable to conceive all her life. And then Gabriel spoke seven of the most wonderful words in the entire Bible: *For with God nothing shall be impossible.*

What happened next was a testament to Mary's character and her utter trust in God. She immediately submitted her will to God, gave up her plans and dreams, and accepted his plan for her life: *I serve you, Lord. I accept that this is your will for my life.* No wonder God was able to trust her with the awesome job of giving birth to his son.

Let's pause here for a moment. It is important to your own theology (what you believe about God) that you get this next part right, because one of the most basic characteristics of God is his eternal being. Mary was the mother of Jesus, and Jesus was God — that's true. But it is incorrect to refer to Mary as the *mother of God.* Think about it:

If God had a mother, he would have a beginning. Having a beginning, of necessity implies having an end. If God had a beginning and an end, he would not be eternal. He would be no more divine than you or I. So we must be careful how we refer to Mary, and what we believe about her.

Just as important is the fact that Mary's husband, Joseph, was not the biological father of Jesus. Joseph was an honorable man, moral, devoted to God and to his future wife. Put yourself in his place. One minute he's anticipating the wonderful life he and Mary are going to have together, and the next he's faced with a life or death decision: *Should he deliver Mary to the high priest for the stoning she so obviously deserved for breaking the Jewish law?* When Mary came to him and told him what the angel Gabriel had told her, Joseph could have reacted several ways.

Although every man and woman since Adam and Eve had been looking forward to the day when the Messiah would deliver them from all their problems, when the announcement finally did arrive, it was a shock. Have you ever anticipated and longed for something so much that when it finally arrived, you had trouble believing it? The Jews had been waiting for the promised Messiah, the deliverer of their atonement with God, for roughly 4,000 years. They knew he would be born of a virgin because the prophet Isaiah had predicted it (Isaiah 7:14), and they knew he would be born in Bethlehem because the prophet Micah had predicted it (Micah 5:2). Every Jew had been taught the prophecies and that the Messiah would fulfill them all. So when Mary turned up pregnant at Joseph's door with a wild tale of an angel telling her she would give birth to the long-awaited Messiah, why wasn't he jumping up and down with happiness? Put yourself in his sandals. How would *you* react if your teenage neighbor knocked on your door and told you she was pregnant with the Savior of the world? Yeah, right.

It was an impossible situation they were in. There was no home pregnancy test available at the local pharmacy, no ultra-sound to prove the pregnancy, and since everyone knew they were in love, who would believe Joseph wasn't the father? From history, we know that Joseph was older than Mary, and from what happened next we know that he loved her very much. So much that when she dropped her bombshell on him, his emotions ran the gamut from fear, worry, astonishment, and shock to joy, exhilaration, awe, a sense of unworthiness and determination to protect her and the child from the misunderstanding and unbelief that would surely dog their lives. Mulling the problem over in his mind, Joseph couldn't bring himself to subject his beloved Mary to the shame and degradation that would surely come when the pregnancy became obvious. All his plans for their life together lay shattered at his feet. So he did what you and I would have done. He took the worst-case scenario Mary had handed him, and opted for Plan B — what he thought was the best solution: he would send Mary out of town, sparing her life.

However, God had a different plan. Emotionally ex-hausted, but at least having made a decision, Joseph finally fell into an uneasy sleep that night. God was aware of Joseph's turmoil, and through a dream, he sent an angel to encourage him. What the angel told him was the best possible news Joseph could have heard: *Don't be afraid to marry Mary and live a normal married life, because the child she is carrying was fathered by God's Holy Spirit. When he is born, call him Jesus, for he shall save his people from their sins.*

Across town, Mary was sleeping peacefully, although it's a

safe bet her parents weren't. Can't you just imagine how they were reacting to Mary's news? *Has she lost her mind? Imagine! Angels appearing to teenagers! What will the neighbors say? We'll be bearing the shame of this all our lives! Is she really pregnant, or is she nuts? How will she ever live this down? She's a good girl — she wouldn't betray Joseph this way. How are we supposed to believe she's going to give birth to the Messiah? Maybe we'd better call off the wedding and send her out of town until this blows over. On the other hand — what if it's really true?*

From our vantage point in the 21 century, we know that it *was* true. Mary of Nazareth, a virgin, gave birth to the Savior of the world. If Mary had not been willing to be used as a channel for blessing the entire human race, and if Joseph had not been willing to go along with her, God would have found another way to fulfill his promise of redemption, of course, because he cannot break a promise. (He wouldn't be God if his word meant nothing.) But God is also omniscient; he knows everything from start to finish before it happens, and he knew how Mary would react to his plan. That's why he chose her before Adam was even created. Mary (and Joseph) knew God well enough to trust him implicitly, even when he turned their lives upside down. Joseph did as God asked, and the wedding date was moved up. It wasn't exactly what they had planned; it was better.

We, too, need to be willing to change our plans to match God's. You never know when God will ask you to do a $180°$ turn and head in the opposite direction. Perhaps the hardest part of changing our plans to conform to his plan is that we often do not know why. Asking *Why, God why?* is a troublesome human trait. We want to be in charge of our lives and make the decisions. Like the toddler who insists *I do it*, we struggle for independence, when all God wants from us is our dependence on him. Thank God for Mary's instant obedience! Because of one teenager's willingness to accept his plan and give up her own, you and I have an invitation to know the eternal, omniscient, omnipresent, and unchangeable God as our Heavenly Father, our Savior, and our closest and most loving friend. He is King of the Universe, and those who believe in him are his children — royalty, with all the privileges and protection that implies.

Mary of Nazareth was just as human and normal as any teenager today, with hopes, dreams, and plans of her own. Then God tapped her on the shoulder and said, *Not that way, this way.* From a humble beginning as an unwed pregnant teenager, she was exalted and blessed above all women. Not because she deserved it, but because she trusted God and said yes to his plan. That's really all God wants any of us to do: believe him.

Mary was given an awesome gift by God. He chose her to give the Messiah a physical presence in the world. Because of her humility, her obedience, and her unshakeable faith in God, every human being — from Adam to those who are yet unborn — has the opportunity to experience eternal life with God. Mary made a choice: *Believe God no matter what the circumstances look like.* You, too, have a choice. You can trust your own instincts, or trust what God has promised you.

Elisabeth
Mother Of A Misfit

By the time we meet Elisabeth, cousin to Mary of Nazareth, in the first chapter of Luke, both she and her husband, Zacharias, are elderly senior citizens, having lived a long and loving life together. Elisabeth and Zacharias were the model couple. He was a priest, and she was descended from Aaron, brother of Moses. They were both devoted to God. The Bible says they were both righteous before God — blameless in his eyes (Luke 1:6). That meant they kept all the commandments God had given to Moses, as well as keeping the hundreds and hundreds of rules the Jewish priests had added with their interpretation of the Mosaic Law. (No easy task!) It must have been a pleasure to visit in their happy home. They were above reproach in every area of their lives — good examples for everyone who knew them.

Yet there was one thing lacking in their lives, and it gave Elisabeth great sadness. They had no children, because Elisabeth had been unable to conceive. (There's that detested word again: *barren*.) We are not told if Elisabeth let that get the best of her, as Hannah did earlier in the Bible. There is every indication that Elisabeth went about her daily life with joy and that she had inner peace about her childlessness. She accepted it as God's will for her life. But somewhere deep inside there must have been an ache that could only be relieved by holding her own baby. Elisabeth was, after all, human. However, God wasn't finished with Elisabeth and Zacharias yet.

One perfectly normal day, while performing his priestly duties at the temple, Zacharias was alone inside the building. An angel appeared to him, just to the right of the altar. Zacharias reacted with fear, wondering what this could mean. (Remember, they didn't have *Touched By An Angel* back then, so they weren't used to seeing angels.) This angel had astounding news. Apparently, Zacharias had never given up on having a child with Elisabeth, and had been praying that God would give them the privilege of being parents. His faith was finally being rewarded. The angel told him Elisabeth would have his son. This son would be named John, and he would be tremendously used by God to prepare the Israelites for their Messiah. The angel said that from the day he was conceived, John would be filled with God's spirit (the Holy Ghost, or Holy Spirit), and that their son would be the means of turning many Israelites back to God. (Throughout history, there have always been people who outwardly worshipped God, but were not really giving him first place in their lives, settling instead for a shallow, impersonal relationship when God was longing to be the most important person in their lives. That is still the case today.)

As dedicated to God as Zacharias was, this news knocked him for a loop. He asked for a sign that it was really true. The angel gave him what he asked for, saying: *I am Gabriel, who stands in the presence of God. Because you doubted what I told you, I'll give you a sign. You will not be able to speak until the day my words come true.* (Not exactly what old Zach had in mind.)

Outside the temple, the congregation had been praying this entire time, and they were wondering what was keeping Zacharias so long. Finally, he emerged. Immediately, they knew something unusual had happened, because he had lost his speech and was using hand signals to communicate with them. He just didn't look the same as before he went in. The people didn't know what to make of it. We're not told if Zacharias explained to them, but it's my guess that he didn't. Somehow, he completed his tour of duty at the temple, remaining speechless, and when his time of service was over, he went home to Elisabeth.

Can you imagine what happened when he got there? *Welcome home, Zach. I missed you.* Silence. *Did you miss me?* Silence. *Zach, what's happened? Why won't you talk to me? You're scaring me!* Silence. And then he painstakingly wrote it all out for her – Gabriel's appearance, the amazing announcement, his doubt and the resulting loss of speech, the promise of a son who would be as powerful as Israel's ancient prophet, Elijah, preparing the way for the long-promised Messiah. Hardly daring to believe what she was reading, it was Elisabeth's turn to be speechless — with joy. It was such an unexpected, tender, loving moment in their long life together that they celebrated with a night of romance. Just before they both fell asleep, Elisabeth knew in her heart of hearts that she was pregnant with their first son. Of all the times they had made love over the years, it had never felt like this. This was different. She fell asleep with a smile on her face, undoubtedly dreaming of knitting little blue booties.

Right away, Elisabeth began wearing looser clothing while her body accommodated itself to the new life within it. Why would she do that before her pregnancy began to show? Luke 1:24 says she hid herself for five months. The Greek word used for *hid* means *to conceal by wrapping and covering over*. It's not that she was ashamed of her growing belly, but rather that she had waited so very long to be pregnant that she wanted to keep it a secret as long as possible, enjoying this time in her life without having to do a lot of explaining. There would be time enough for sharing her son later.

When Elisabeth was six months into her pregnancy, her teenage cousin Mary of Nazareth showed up at her door for an unexpected visit. The same exact moment Elisabeth heard Mary's greeting, her baby kicked the side of her womb. She was so overcome with the joy of God's Holy Spirit that she burst out in praise to God with a loud voice. Remember now that Elisabeth had *not* been told that Mary was pregnant. The cousins lived in different parts of Israel, and the last she had heard, Mary and Joseph were just engaged, not married. The angel, Gabriel, had told Mary that Elisabeth was six months pregnant when he had appeared to her revealing that she would give birth to the Messiah. Another miracle! In his tender love for Mary, knowing it would be hard for her to process all that was happening to her, God gave her a confidante who truly understood the miracle that was happening. (God made women with a special need for girlfriends, I think. No man can really understand what a woman goes through when she's pregnant. It's a special sisterhood.)

Mary had been told that Elisabeth was six months pregnant, but she didn't know that the baby would become John, the Baptist, the one who would prepare the way for Israel's Messiah. It's a testimony to God's attention to detail, his perfect timing in the lives of those who love him, that he gave these two cousins the special joy of being pregnant at the same time. What a support system! Mary stayed with Elisabeth and Zacharias for three months, and then she went home to Joseph. Remember, Mary was around fourteen years old at this time. The time with Elisabeth had prepared her for the physical changes that were happening to her body, and for the spiritual changes that were on the horizon. But neither woman had a clue that both of their sons would be the source of great joy as well as great sorrow in their lives. God does not usually reveal his entire plan to us, only what we need to know for the moment. There are at least two reasons for that: he wants us to trust him implicitly. If we knew the entire plan, we wouldn't need to trust; and if we knew the difficulties that lay ahead of us, we would be overwhelmed. Elisabeth would have been distraught if she had known ahead of time that her darling baby boy would eventually be beheaded by Herod.

God is never surprised by what happens in our lives. If he didn't know everything there was to know, he wouldn't be God. If you have given your life to God, it is important to remember that every single thing (both the good and the seemingly bad) that happens to you is first allowed by God. Just as a coffee filter allows the water to flow through the coffee grounds, but keeps the grounds in the filter, God allows certain events and certain people to pass through his loving hands into the lives of his children, and keeps others from touching us. Sad, but true, not everyone is born a child of God. Yes, we are all his children in the general sense that he created us, but the rules changed when first Eve, and then Adam, chose to doubt what God had told them and violated the only rule he had given them. (*Don't eat that one particular fruit.*) Since that pivotal moment in the history of humanity, the only way to be a spiritual child of God has been to accept his provision for reconciliation: the promised Messiah. For the person whose soul and spirit has been reconciled to God, that protection is in place: everything is *Father-filtered*, even what appears to be bad.

Elisabeth's baby had a very difficult assignment from God.

Exactly how does one person go about convincing a whole nation that the one event they have been eagerly awaiting for thousands of years is finally here? John was not only cousin to Jesus, he was also his point man. Because of the period of history in which both John and Jesus lived, the Jews were particularly desperate for someone to rescue them from the dominancy of the Roman Empire. As it was in the days of Moses, Israel was looking for a physical deliverance from the tyranny imposed upon them. They wanted the hated Romans out. Immediately wouldn't have been soon enough. They needed deliverance right then, and they looked to their promised Messiah to provide it. They had their emPHAsis on the wrong syLAble! But understandably so. That is why they were so confused when John, the Baptist, began preaching repentance and the spiritual deliverance that was at hand. Focused on the Roman tyranny, they had their own idea of what the Messiah was going to do for them. And it had nothing to do with repentance.

John did not turn out to be the type of son Elisabeth and Zacharias had anticipated. The Gospels describe him as a wild man, full of spit and vinegar, afraid of no one and nothing — except displeasing God. We are not told when or how it happened, but there came a time in his life when John knew exactly why he had been born. His one purpose in life was to tell the world that the Messiah had come. And he told them with every eccentric bone in his body. This was a man whose main diet was locusts and honey, whose entire wardrobe was a camel's hair tunic, a wide leather belt, and sandals. To say he was a nonconformist is to put it mildly. He never shaved, never used Old Spice, and didn't give a hoot about Blackwell's best-dressed list. He had a mission, and he gave it every ounce of his concentration and strength. The rest of it was inconsequential. Hardly the son Liz and Zach had envisioned! (If your teenager isn't exactly what you expected, take heart.)

It must have been particularly difficult for Elisabeth to watch her only child become the object of ridicule as he plunged wholeheartedly into his ministry. She was so very proud of him — why couldn't others see how wonderful he was? Through all the growing up years, John was always odd-man out with the other children, except his cousin, Jesus, who lived miles away. Alternately diagnosed as moody, psychotic, and dangerous, John would have been a very lonely boy if God had not revealed his greater purpose for his life. Yes, John was a misfit in every sense of the word. Zacharias must have wanted his son to follow in his footsteps and enter the priesthood. Early on, Elisabeth must have been dreaming of the grandchildren she would undoubtedly spoil one day. Eventually, it became evident to John's parents that this was no ordinary child they had brought into the world. That was a hard pill to swallow. All their married lives they had been different because they were childless. Now they had a child who caused people to shake their heads and feel sorry for his parents. It was a cross they bore stoically, but it was a cross, nonetheless.

Jesus, of course, knew what John's mission in life was, and he loved and respected his cousin tremendously. There had never been a child like John in the history of the world, nor has there been one like him since the day he died. He was totally unique. Jesus said he was the greatest man who had ever lived (Matthew 11:11). From our standpoint two thousand years later, we would label John a wild man. But, knowing what we know, it's easy to see why John had to be the way he was. God had to whip the Israelites into shape for the coming Messiah, and he used John to do it.

But for Elisabeth in particular, watching her son make both converts and enemies with his incessant message of repentance had to have been extremely difficult. She and Zacharias had had such dreams for their little boy! But he turned out to be the worst kind of oddball — always in trouble and causing an uproar everywhere he went. We must remember, however, that God had prepared Elisabeth's heart for this in those early pregnant days when she stayed close to home and communed with him. She had been told that John would be a lot like the feisty ancient prophet, Elijah. But still, watching her son become the brunt of jokes and the often-unwelcome outspoken messenger of God tore her heart apart. Knowing it in her head and living with it every day were two different scenarios.

What do you do when your child doesn't fulfill your expectations? The one thing that keeps a parent focused is the love for the child. Under it all, there is the love. As parents, we need to realize that each child belongs to God, and that we only have that child in trust, for a short time. It's easy to transfer our own expectations and goals onto our children's lives, especially if we were not able to achieve them ourselves. However, it's important to keep in mind that God has an individual plan for each child who comes into the world. And it probably isn't the same plan we have in mind as parents.

A parent's mission is to nurture, protect, provide for, guide and teach each child not only what he or she needs to know to survive to adulthood, but also to develop character and a healthy relationship with God. A child's spiritual development is every bit as important to his or her success as food and clothing. God gives us whole children (body, soul and spirit), and expects us to raise them into the adults he can use to bless the world and achieve his purpose for their lives. It may be hard to accept, but there comes a time when each parent must give each child back to God. (Jesus didn't exactly fit the mold, either.) Elisabeth and Zacharias had a son who turned out to be the biggest misfit in history. It was hard on them, and hard on their son. John the Baptist carried out his commission from God extremely well, but his faithfulness cost him his head. It's hard to imagine the co-mingling of agony and awe Elisabeth and Zacharias experienced when their beloved only son was so cruelly killed.

All they could do was their best, love each other, and trust God. When it comes right down to it, that's all any parent can do. We are all works in progress.

Anna
Never Too Old To Be Used

Eight days after Mary of Nazareth gave birth, in keeping with the Law of Moses, the baby was circumcised and was named *Jesus*, as Gabriel had told them. The law was very specific in all things, and thirty-three days after the circumcision, it was time for Mary to make an offering at the temple. The forty-day period from the birth was a time set aside for Mary to regain her strength and get used to being a mother, a special bonding time. After the offering, Mary would be considered purified from the childbirth, and could then participate in normal worship and activities. But for Mary (and Joseph), life would never be normal again.

The Jewish law stated that every first-born male child was considered dedicated to God, so it was a proud moment when Joseph and Mary arrived at the temple in Jerusalem, carrying Jesus. This was the first time their boy would be in the temple, a place that had very special meaning in every Jewish boy's life, but especially so for this little one. Remember now, Jesus' parents knew he was the Messiah, but they really didn't know how that was going to play out in their lives. They were full of anticipation and hope and trust in God to somehow make this child the salvation of Israel, but they had no clue how it was going to happen.

One of the first people Mary and Joseph met when they arrived at the temple was a gentle, elderly woman named Anna. Here was a woman whose heart was in tune with the Spirit of God. She had been married when she was around Mary's age, but after seven years, her husband died unexpectedly. As anyone would be, Anna was devastated. Gone were her dreams, her happy life, and her beloved husband. What was she supposed to do with the rest of her life? It would have been both logical and probable that she would marry a second time and live out a normal life. But God had another path laid out for Anna.

Shortly after her husband's funeral, Anna began spending every waking minute at the temple, praying and worshipping God. When you spend a lot of time with a person, it's inevitable that some of that person's character rubs off on you. That's why it's so important to choose your companions well. We learn something from everyone we spend time with. God taught Anna a lot about himself in those first difficult months of her widowhood. He comforted her in her grief, and provided solace and hope.   The more time Anna spent in God's presence, the more she realized that she was destined to remain a widow, devoting her life to God and whatever he wanted her to do. For eighty-four years, Anna did exactly that. She moved into the temple and became a blessing to everyone she met. She accepted her assignment from God; she didn't fight it.

By the time Mary and Joseph carried the infant Jesus up the temple steps, Anna was well over 100 years old. Luke 2:37 says she praised and worshipped God day and night, never leaving the temple. If this had happened in the 21 century, we would assume Anna was overcome with grief and had withdrawn from the world. If there had been a convent where she could have gone into seclusion, she would have been there. It's important to *not* think of Anna as a recluse, out of touch with reality. Everyone deals with grief in his or her own way, and somehow, everyone gets through it. Anna grieved for her husband, of course, but not for 84 years. This woman was no basket case. At some point, the grief morphed into acceptance of a new and higher calling on Anna's life. She had gone to the temple in despair; she stayed to serve in joy.

The second Anna saw Jesus, she knew who he was. God's spirit within her literally jumped for joy, and Anna immediately offered a prayer of thanksgiving to God. She didn't stop there, though. From that moment on, she told everyone within hearing distance that God's promised redemption had arrived. She was the very first person to tell people Jesus was the Christ, which is exactly what God is still asking each of us to do. If you have placed your faith in God, and have asked him to use you, he will. It may be baking a loaf of bread for a busy young mother who lives down the street, or it may be driving an elderly neighbor to the grocery store. It may be spending an hour praying for the rebellious teenager across the street who is headed for serious trouble. The only question you have to answer is, *Am I willing for God to use me?* If you are, he will. Count on it. And make sure you have your running shoes on!

Unlike America, God doesn't put a person out to pasture at retirement age. (Personally, I cannot find a basis anywhere in the Bible for retirement as we think of it in this country.) But if you do retire *from* something, you have to retire *to* something. Something has to fill the empty hours, or (in the case of the death of a loved one), something has to fill the empty place in the heart. Isn't it wonderful that you're never too old to be used by God? Granted, you may never be an Anna or a Mother Teresa, but if you are a woman of a certain age (to put it gently), you still have the rest of your life ahead of you — however long that may be. A wise woman asks God to use her to bless others, and then expects him to reveal countless opportunities to her each and every day.

If you are widowed, or divorced, or if you have never married, you can experience a deeply satisfying life full of peace, joy, love, and laughter. Personally, I've been single all my life except for a brief eleven month marriage, so I speak from experience when I say that it's possible to be a serenely spiritual woman, no matter what happens to you. On days when circumstances try to overwhelm you, offer him praise that life isn't a parade passing you by. Don't be a Pollyanna, but look for the positive side of every negative. (Trust me. There's one there somewhere!) Identify some little thing to be thankful for. Center your life on him. Keep your heart, soul and spirit focused on what has eternal value, and he will use you to tell people about his love — just as he used Anna to tell anyone who would listen that Jesus was the promised Messiah. Unlike Anna, you may not have another 84 years ahead of you, but whatever amount of time God does give you, you can give it back to him. Remember that famous line: *It's not over until it's over.*

Martha and Mary

The Unbalanced Sister Act

There is a big gap in the Bible about Jesus' childhood and teen-age years. Why didn't God tell us more? I believe it is because we are not supposed to get sidetracked on unimportant details and miss the real message. Because Jesus was both divine and human at the same time (a very difficult concept for us to understand), he had to experience the normal growing up problems we all face. I'm sure he fell off his bike and skinned his knees. I'm sure he made mistakes on his math and spelling tests. I'm sure the other kids teased him and made him the butt of their jokes. Otherwise, how would he ever understand how we feel when those things happen to us? Hebrews 4:15 says, *He understands our weaknesses and was tempted in every way that we are tempted.* What a comfort! He really does understand our daily struggles. It would be hard to have a God who couldn't relate.

Every human being needs friends, and Jesus was no exception. By the time he was thirty-something he had surrounded himself with the twelve disciples, and an inner circle of friends who loved him. There were three friends who were closer to him than most: Lazarus of Bethany, and his two sisters, Mary and Martha. Bethany was a quiet little village just under two miles from Jerusalem, so during his three-year itinerant ministry, Jesus spent a lot of time with these three people. He felt at home with them, and genuinely loved them and enjoyed their company. The feeling was mutual. A true friend is someone who knows the worst about you and loves you anyway. Lazarus, Mary, and Martha were free to be themselves with Jesus, and, more importantly, in their home he was free to be himself. As good friends do, they provided shelter, food, and companionship. They earned the right to know a side of Jesus that most never saw.

Mary and Martha approached life from two different perspectives. Martha was capable, efficient, competent, sensible and practical. She always saw what had to be done and did it well. (We all know someone like that, right?) Mary, on the other hand, was the one most likely to stop and smell the roses. She did her share of work around the house, but her mind was more apt to be focused on how the dust particles sparkled in the sunlight rather than on the dusting. Could two sisters be any more opposite?

Martha was probably a widow, because the house was referred to as being hers and there is no mention of a husband. (Most women in that time were either married or still living in their fathers' homes.) As Martha bustled about the kitchen, preparing the meal, planning the seating arrangement, pressing the best linen tablecloth, and timing the roast precisely so it would be ready when the vegetables were perfectly cooked, Mary was sitting at Jesus' feet, hanging on his every word.

Why can't she see the things that need to be done before we can eat? Martha fumed silently. *It would be a fine mess if I left the kitchen and went and sat at Jesus' feet like she does! I love him, too, but someone has to feed this crowd.* She stewed and muttered until she couldn't stand it another minute. She went into the courtyard and spoke sharply to Jesus. *Lord, don't you care that Mary isn't helping me prepare the meal for this crowd? Tell her to come and help me!* Jesus was in a ticklish situation. He loved both Mary and Martha, and he was well aware of the work involved in preparing a big meal, because he had helped his mother enough to understand it. He was, however, a master teacher, and this was an opportunity to teach an important lesson.

Martha could have used a lesson in priority setting, and Mary would have benefited from a lesson in responsibility, but that's not what Jesus zeroed in on. With love in his eyes and his voice, he spoke gently to Martha, and the anger and resentment left her. *Martha, Martha, you're careful and troubled about many things. Only one thing is necessary, and Mary has figured out what that is. I won't take it away from her.* What did he mean?

Martha had a wonderful reputation as a homemaker and hostess. No detail escaped her notice and everything she did, she did with excellence. Nothing was too good for her guests. When she threw a party, her crystal sparkled, the water goblets, wine goblets and silverware were in exactly the right places, and the tablecloth was whiter than white with the creases in exactly the right places. She always folded her napkins into fancy shapes and when she called her guests to the table, she expected them to drop everything and come *immediately.* After all, she had worked hard to have everything just right; the least they could do is sit down on time. (If that scenario sounds familiar, listen up!)

The Greek word Jesus used for *careful* means *to be anxious about* — *anxious to the point of distraction.* The Greek word Jesus used for *troubled* means *to make something troubled or to disturb something.* Martha couldn't leave well enough alone when it came to her reputation for doing things right. She consistently went overboard on things that didn't really matter in the light of eternity. Those of us who have perfectionist tendencies can relate to Martha very well. What we don't want people to know is that we really feel inadequate in some way, and perfectionism is our way of covering that up. We don't know what was really bothering Martha. Maybe Mary was younger and prettier. Maybe Martha wasn't as bright as she thought she should be. Maybe she felt the only thing she did well was keep house, so she was going to excel at that, even if it killed her. Whatever was driving her, it was out of proportion. Mary, on the other hand, couldn't drag herself away from Jesus' side. Hanging on his every word, an ecstatic smile on her face, she simply glowed with happiness. And it drove Martha crazy.

One thing these two women had in common, however, was their deep love for Jesus and a firm belief that he was the Messiah, the Son of God. When Jesus spoke, Martha really listened. With his piercing look into her eyes as he responded to her demand that he make Mary help her, he saw straight into her heart of hearts, and something in Martha breathed a sigh of relief and nestled down. It was okay. He knew how she felt and he loved her anyway. She didn't have to be the perfect hostess. She only had to love him, let him love her, and everything would turn out just fine. In that one moment of time, she reordered her priorities.

Later, when their brother, Lazarus, died unexpectedly and Jesus took six days to get there, it was Martha who ran to meet him as he approached the house while Mary sat inside, depressed and discouraged. It was practical Martha to whom Jesus said, "I am the resurrection and the life: he that believeth in me, though he were dead, yet shall he live." When Jesus asked if she believed him, it was no-nonsense, factual Martha who gave the passionate response, "Yes, Lord: I believe you are the Christ, the Son of God...." And then she went to tell her sister that Jesus had come. Martha had learned that when Jesus is present in a life, everything else falls into the proper perspective.

Thank God he doesn't put people in boxes labeled *pushy*, *selfish*, or *not-too-bright*! He deals with each of us as individuals. He knows our deepest secrets and our worst fears, our burning desires and our greatest needs. Mary of Bethany had a tremendous spiritual sensitivity, with an accompanying capacity for both the highest of highs and the lowest of lows. What she needed was balance. What did Jesus mean when he said Mary had grasped the most important thing? I believe he was referring to Mary's focus on God's place in her life. She made spiritual things her number one priority. She didn't get rattled when her paycheck was late and it looked as if she wouldn't be able to make her mortgage payment on time. She wasn't concerned when gasoline prices crept higher and higher and a trip to the local supermarket took more money than she had budgeted. She just continued trusting God to meet her needs, and everything always worked out. Instead of worrying that the napkins at each place were folded just so, she did well to remember to put the package of napkins on the table!

Jesus was not saying, however, that Mary was perfect. If your head is always in the clouds, your feet are bound to trip over something on your path. God doesn't intend for us to go through life with blinders on. I know I've said this before, but it bears repeating: *You can be so heavenly minded, you're no earthly good!* The point Jesus was making was this: *Mary had her priorities straight.* If we put God first, everything else will fall into place, and we will have tremendous peace and happiness in this life. Some of us never learn that lesson. Mary knew that Martha was capable of doing everything without her help. If Martha had gently tapped Mary on the shoulder and asked her to lend a hand, Mary would have done it gladly, because she loved her sister. It just never occurred to her to offer.

When Lazarus died, and Jesus raised him from the dead, both Mary and Martha were speechless with joy and awe. This display of his awesome power thrilled them both and confirmed once again that Jesus was, indeed, God. True to her nature, Mary felt impelled to express her adoration for the rest of Jesus' earthly life. She expressed it at every opportunity, and in many ways that were both common and uncommon practice in that culture and time: sitting at his feet as he taught, anointing his head with costly ointment, and anointing his feet with perfume, mingled with her tears of gratitude for what he had done for her, and wiping off his feet with her hair. She gave Jesus the best she had, and demonstrated her devotion in every way she knew. Others criticized her extravagance in using an entire pound of expensive ointment in this way, but she didn't care. Jesus understood her heart, and praised her for her senseless acts of love. How could he react otherwise?

Both Mary and Martha needed balance in their lives. When the Spirit of God enters a life, he levels out the spikes and dips in our personalities — with love — making us more like we were intended to be. It isn't life itself that makes us out of balance; it's how we react to it that determines our peace and joy. If God is working on a particular area of your life that needs tempering, don't fight it. Let him do whatever it is he's trying to accomplish in you. He has your eternal happiness in mind. Trust him with that, and with your daily ups and downs as well. Learn the lessons Martha and Mary learned in his presence.

Couldn't He Have Found Another Way?

It is very difficult to understand why God couldn't have found another way to rescue us from the penalty of our willful disobedience (otherwise known as sin). Since he is all-knowing and all-powerful, was it really *necessary* for Jesus to die in such a horrible way?

Yes. It was. Here's why.

Jesus was born to die. That was his entire purpose for coming into this world. In the beginning, God had set up one rule with our ancestors in the Garden of Eden. It was the only requirement he made of them. When they knowingly disobeyed him, they violated the covenant he had made with them. Because God is pure and holy, it is not possible for him to overlook willful disobedience. (As parents, we shouldn't overlook it in our children, either.) Also because he is pure and holy, the only way to restore the broken relationship between himself and man was for God to take the initiative and make things right again. If there was going to be complete and total reconciliation, it had to come from him. So he took the initiative and made a way for us to be restored: by faith in the way he himself would provide.

The way God provided for mankind to be reconciled again was through an innocent sacrifice. Someone had to pay the penalty for breaking the law God had laid down. Yes, you're right. The logical choice would have been Adam and Eve. They are the ones who should have been sacrificed. But then, where would you and I be? (Not here, that's for sure!)

Because God loved Adam and Eve so very much, be decided to pay the penalty himself. That's why the omnipotent, omniscient, loving God became a little baby boy in Bethlehem two thousand years later. God became a man, so he himself could be the innocent sacrifice required to obliterate man's sin forever.

The baby born to Mary was God incarnate (in the flesh). There was no other way.

Thirty-three years later, when that baby had grown into a man, his body hung on a rough wooden cross while the life poured out of his wounds. There was only one reason why he was even there: *love. He died for love.* Love for you, and me, and every human being who has ever lived or who will ever live. As his innocent blood stained the dirt at the foot of his cross, the stain of man's sin disappeared.

No, I don't really understand it all. Yes, I believe it with all my mind and heart. Why? Because God is smarter than I am, and everything he has said has worked out to be true. He knows the end from the beginning; I don't. And to tell the truth, I don't want to. It's far easier to just believe what he has told us, accept what he has done to remedy the situation, and to trust him implicitly – for both this life, and the life to come. Believing and trusting him gives me peace, joy, and hope. Why would I give that up to try some other solution that might or might not work? I, for one, am sticking with what I know works.

Mary Magdalene
A Liberated Woman

It's not easy to be misunderstood and lied about. Since medieval times, Mary of Magdala has been typecast as a prostitute. I remember being taught that she was a bad woman who sold her body to whichever man could pay the price. I am older now, and I have searched the Greek passages about Mary Magdalene for myself, and I find no evidence of that anywhere in Scripture. All the Bible says about this Mary's past is that she had been healed of evil spirits and infirmities and that she had had seven devils. What exactly is a *devil*?

The Greek word used in reference to Mary's problems in Luke 8:2 means a *supernatural spirit of a bad nature.* Most of what we call *personal demons* today - alcoholism, guilt, drug addiction, depression, suicidal tendencies, addiction to sex, kleptomania – are not the same thing that Mary of Magdala was dealing with. She had problems, probably more than most people, or at least her problems were more visible. We aren't told what her problems were. Whatever they were, they made her an outcast. Misunderstood, mistrusted, the butt of busybodies' gossip and the town joke: She must have been miserable. If ever anyone was a candidate for a healing touch from God, it was Mary of Magdala.

Comedian Flip Wilson used to make us laugh by saying, "The devil made me do it." He said it so often, it became a household phrase all across America. You may not believe there is a devil (the spiritual evil being we refer to as Satan). God did not create evil. What he *did* create was an angel named Lucifer (which means *clear brightness*). Lucifer had the ability to choose either good or evil, just as you and I do. He chose evil. (For a bright creature, that was a very stupid move.) Since then, he has been known as Satan (which means *to attack or accuse*) — the archenemy of good. Personally, I believe that since there is light, the opposite is possible: dark. Since there is good, the opposite is possible: evil. It makes sense. (I also believe that Flip was wrong: the devil cannot *make* you do anything. But we'll get to that in a minute.)

One day as Mary hung around the fringes of the crowd that had gathered to hear Jesus teach, he looked at her, and saw through to her soul. He saw her faith in him, and her misery and the anguish in her heart. He had compassion on her, and he healed her. The devilish spirits left her, and her spirit soared, free at last. From that moment forward, Mary Magdalene was a liberated woman.

In the latter half of the twentieth century, *liberated* came to mean something totally different. That's not what we're talking about here. Mary's was a *spiritual* liberation. To be truly liberated means to be set free: free from self-condemnation, loosed from any bonds that were holding you back, free to be all God intended you to be, free to love yourself and those around you, free to laugh at yourself when you make a mistake, free to enjoy life. Mary's gratitude was so great, so overwhelming, that she became one of Jesus' closest followers. He had given her back her dignity; how could she *not* give him her life?

Throughout the rest of the Bible's account of Jesus' ministry, Mary Magdalene is mentioned often. She was with him for three major events: his crucifixion, burial, and resurrection. It was Mary who first discovered that the huge stone sealing Jesus' tomb had been rolled aside. Immediately she ran to tell the disciples, who ran back with her to the tomb. They left, but Mary stayed, crying her heart out. Her tears of sorrow turned into tears of joy, however, because Jesus appeared to her, alive again, as he had promised. Mary's heart sang with joy. It was true! There was hope for everyone, because Jesus had defeated the last enemy — death.

No longer did people have to be afraid to die. No longer did they have to await God's redemption. It had arrived, in the person of Jesus, the Christ. The long-awaited Messiah. Her loving Lord. Her Savior and Redeemer. Because the resurrection of Jesus defeated man's last enemy, death was no longer *terminal*;

it became *transitional*.

When he told her to go and tell the others that he had risen from the dead, as he had promised, was it any wonder that her feet seemed to have wings and her heart beat faster with excitement as she ran to tell everyone what had happened? It seems like some sort of divine justice that it was a woman who was entrusted with that joyous mission. We have no more information on Mary's life after that first Easter morning, but we can safely assume that until the day she died, she continued to tell everyone who would listen about the wonderful things God had done for her.

Throughout the Old Testament women are true heroes in the history of Israel (Deborah, for one). God chose women to bear children, not men. God liberated women forever when he chose a woman (Mary of Nazareth) to give birth to his son. It was a woman (Anna) who first proclaimed to the world that Jesus was the Messiah. It was the women who fed him and provided clean sheets for him to sleep on (Mary and Martha of Bethany). It was the women who stood at the foot of his cross, unashamed to be counted as his followers. It was the women who anointed his body for burial. It was the women who witnessed his burial. It was a woman (Mary Magdalene) who was the first person to see the risen Christ. She was also the first to tell the world that he was alive again, in effect becoming the first New Testament missionary.

Inequality between the sexes is not a biblical concept. Jesus completely accepted and appreciated women — in full equality with men. He respected them, enjoyed being around them, and treated them the same way he treated men. He was just as quick to point out a problem in a man's life as he was to point out a problem in a woman's life. Nowhere in the Bible is there any evidence to the contrary. He treated everyone the same – with love and respect, and fairness.

Salome
Blinded By Ambition

Salome's (Sal-OH-mee) claim to fame was the fact that two of her sons were chosen by Jesus to be part of his twelve disciples. James and John were part of Jesus' inner circle of friends and traveled with him throughout his three-year ministry here. Some Bible scholars believe she was Jesus' aunt, the sister of Mary of Nazareth; others disagree. It really doesn't matter if she was related to him or not. What's important is the lesson we can learn from her.

Every mother has dreams for her children. That's normal. It's also not unusual for parents to want to project their unfulfilled dreams onto their children. Salome was not simply ambitious for her sons to have fame and glory; she was zealous in the pursuit of her goal. And that's where she made her mistake. She nursed her completely human ambition until she embarrassed herself with it.

What Salome wanted was prestige for her boys. And she wanted it *now*. An acknowledgement by Jesus that they would have their reward in Heaven would pay off in spades in the present. After all, they had left their careers to follow Jesus, and she wanted them to be richly rewarded for their dedication and sacrifice. Anyone who has ever been a parent knows the feeling of pride when a child does something wonderful. It's not only pride in the child, it's also pride in the family gene pool. *That's my kid! Isn't he great? Didn't I do a good job raising him? The apple doesn't fall far from the tree, does it now?* These are the thoughts Salome had hoarded in her heart until they compelled her to ask Jesus for a personal favor.

Jesus had been spending quality time with the twelve,

explaining to them God's plan for the world, and for them as individuals. They had witnessed everything he said and did, and they had questions. Small wonder! Their Messiah wasn't anything like what they had expected, and they were having difficulty getting a grip on the application of it all. In fairness to Salome, even that great pillar of Christianity, Peter, had asked Jesus what his reward was going to be for giving up everything to follow him. (Matthew 19:27)

From every viewpoint, Salome's boys were great. It took guts to leave everything behind and follow Jesus. But instead of keeping her pride in them to herself, she wanted public acknowledgment. She confused worldly acclaim with greatness. She wanted the world to know James and John were better than the other disciples, and that they would be rewarded by being given positions of honor in Heaven, one on Jesus' left, and one on Jesus' right. This is what she asked when she knelt before Jesus. Her sons were there too, kneeling with her, fully aware of what she was asking and coveting the prestige for themselves. (Mark 10:35-40) These three didn't need assertiveness training! From a human standpoint, this was definitely the way to get ahead in life. Spiritually, however, it was the worst thing they could have done.

Jesus answered Salome's request with a firm, but gentle, reprimand. *You don't know what you're asking. This favor is not mine to grant.* (Did she really think he'd say, *Okay. The seats are theirs?*) Immediately, but too late, she realized she had been out of line. Then he added, *Whoever wants to be great, should be the servant of all.*

Ouch! Salome might have been pushy, but she wasn't stupid. Still on her knees, she thought, *What have I done? How could I have been so blinded by my own ambition for my sons? I gave them to God when they were born, after all. It's just that I want the very best for them. Does that make me a bad mother?* No, it just made her human. Lowering her head in dismay, Salome fought tears. She could hear the people around Jesus, especially his disciples, muttering under their breath, indignant at her request. Once again (for the umpteenth time), she figuratively placed her sons' lives on the altar of her heart and offered them to God. *You have a plan for Jimmy and Johnny, Lord, and I have no right to interfere. Forgive me. You know best. You pick their seats in Heaven. It's okay with me.* She still held them tightly in her heart, but she held them with an open palm. (That is the *only* way to keep what you don't want to lose.)

From that point on, Salome showed her own greatness by continuing to be one of Jesus' most devoted and faithful followers. She was there at the foot of the cross, and she was one of the women who went to the tomb to anoint his body, but found the tomb empty instead. She made a mistake in asking Jesus to honor her sons above all others, but she accepted his rebuke gracefully, and didn't let it keep her from growing spiritually. That shows her greatness of spirit.

True greatness (spiritual or otherwise) is not a thing to be *given*. It has to come from inside the character and spirit of a person. It has to manifest itself in a thousand little ways in everyday, trying circumstances. It's been said that true character is what you are when you are alone and the lights are out. True greatness is determined by a person's value system. The most important thing parents can do for their children is plant seeds of greatness while their fertile minds and spirits are soft and receptive, and nurture them with love, discipline, and right thinking. The seeds of responsibility, creativity, perseverance, integrity, wisdom, faith, adaptability and self-esteem are essentials of greatness. You cannot go out and purchase them with your Visa or MasterCard. They are gifts from God — seeds he has planted in each human being's life. He expects you to cultivate them in your children...and in yourself. The rewards of doing so are both immediate and eternal. Humility is the path to greatness. The way *up*, is *down*.

Samantha
Right Church. Wrong Pew.

Every so often, there is a single moment in life that completely changes a person. These moments are frozen in time and memory, and act as a watershed experience, separating everything that came before from everything that comes after. They become crystal-clear pivot points, sparkling with clarity and meaning. Viewed in retrospect, they explain a person's life and define his or her character. One such moment was when the Samaritan woman met Jesus at the well. For the purposes of this story (and since we don't know her name), let's call her Samantha.

In a not-so-great period of Israel's history, Omri (OM-ree), a not-so-great king of Israel, bought a hill from a man and named it Samaria. The Bible describes him as the worst king Israel had had up to that time.

Omri was a military leader and both he and his henchmen actively looked for ways to turn the people against God. Omri and his people had picked up the ways of the world down through their generations, and what had evolved was a watered-down version of Judaism that really didn't do a thing for them, except make them feel complacent. They even built a temple to rival the one in Jerusalem. Their brand of religion had very little left in it to make it recognizable as the faith of Abraham, Moses and David. Consequently, the people in Samaria did not follow the same moral code as the rest of the Jews. They allowed graven images for example, which was in direct disobedience to Mosaic Law, but that is only one of the many reasons for the hatred between the two groups.

106

For six of Omri's twelve years as king, Samaria was his capital city. Always known for its low level of living, in Jesus' day Samaria was the equivalent of the red-light district, where prostitution was openly practiced and the money earned went into vineyards and groves of fig trees which produced even more income. It was ill-gotten gain, but when morality goes out the window, a false prosperity often prevails. People went to the temple, and practiced their brand of religion, but it was a far cry from what the God of Israel had commanded them through Moses.

For these reasons, the road to Samaria was an unpopular one for Jews, and they avoided it whenever possible. The Samaritans had a bad reputation that was thousands of years old, and the old hatred for the Samaritans still smoldered in the hearts of the Jews when Jesus walked the Earth. One day while walking to Galilee from Judea, Jesus stopped to rest in a field, at a well that had belonged to Jacob thousands of years before.

As he sat there, a woman from the nearby village approached the well to fill her water jug. One look at Jesus told her he was a Jew, and immediately her defenses went up. It was just Samantha's luck that someone was at the well at this hour. She had trudged in the brutal sun over the dry, dusty trail to the well, carefully timing her arrival at midday, when most people would be inside their homes, not out in the hottest part of the day. She was not only tired from being up all night, earning money from prostituting herself, but she was also weary in her spirit, desperately weary. She was no longer a young woman. How much longer could she keep up this lifestyle? (When things are not right in a person's spirit, the body and the soul are not right either.) All she wanted to do was fill her jug and trudge home so she could take a nap before starting work again that night. The night shift was a killer! As she glanced at Jesus, she thought, *He looks like a Jew, so maybe he won't speak to me and I can get my water and get out of here. I hope he doesn't want to make an appointment with me. I am totally booked for the next month. He looks like a gentle man, but you can never tell. Men usually want only one thing from a woman, and I'm fresh out of that today.*

Unbelievably the man did speak to her, asking her for a

drink of water. Samantha's mind reacted. *This man's not as bright as he looks. What's wrong with him?* Then she answered him with, *Don't you know that Jews have no dealings with Samaritans?* His reply confused her. *If you knew who was speaking to you, you would have asked me for a drink instead, and I would have given you living water.* Wary now, and feeling an unexpected tugging on her heartstrings, she asked him how he expected to get a drink when he had nothing to haul the water up from the deep well. And what did he mean by living water and where did it come from? Jesus answered, "Whoever drinks of the water I give him, will never thirst, but will have a well of water inside him springing up into eternal life."

What? As Samantha gaped at him, the tugging on her heartstrings turned into a strong pull on her spirit. Suddenly, she wasn't so weary. In the midst of her hopelessness, hope began to bubble up inside her. *Maybe there was a way out, after all!* She still did not fully comprehend what Jesus was really saying. As he looked directly into her eyes, the strengthening pull on her spirit swelled into an undeniable demand. Whatever this living water was, she wanted it. Samantha took the first step in her redemption, and *asked* Jesus to help her. She asked him to give her the living water, so she would not be thirsty or have to draw water from the well again. She missed the point, but her needy spirit responded to his offer.

Jesus zeroed in on the bottom line. He told Samantha to go home and bring her husband back with her. He had tapped her sleeping conscience on the shoulder and it forced her to make a choice. She decided to level with him, and responded that she had no husband. Jesus recognized her choice to be honest with him — and with herself as well. He responded, "What you say is true; you've had five husbands, and the man you're with now is not your husband." Astonished, Samantha knew in her heart that this was the most important moment in her life. How she reacted now would determine the course of the rest of her life. Samantha knew her lifestyle was not pleasing to God. Jesus didn't have to lay a guilt trip on her; she did it herself. He didn't censure her; he simply stated the facts. Somehow, her conscience had survived, and in his presence, it convicted her.

Knowing that he had her complete attention, Jesus said, "God is a spirit, and those who worship him must worship him in spirit and in truth." Jesus knew that the people of Samaria had a form of religion, but didn't really know (or even *desire* to know) the truth about God. There is a difference between religion and Christianity. One is man's attempt to reach God. The other is God's attempt to reach man. What Jesus was saying to Samantha was that God wanted her entire life — spirit, soul, and body — her spiritual core, her mind, emotions and will, and her physical self. She had asked him for a quick fix for her physical need for water, and he had offered her a permanent solution to all her needs: a relationship with God for all eternity. (It never ceases to amaze me that God is always ready to give us so much more than we can even imagine! Why do we insist on living in spiritual poverty when God's desire is to heap his immeasurable love and blessings on us?)

Her water jug forgotten, her tired feet tingling with energy, her weary eyes alight with hope, she turned and ran back to her village to tell everyone who would listen that she had met the Christ, the promised Messiah from God. So great was the change in her, the people of Samaria paid attention to her and many went to see Jesus for themselves. Their response to his message of redemption was so great that Jesus and his disciples stayed there for two days, teaching them. Samantha had accepted Jesus for who he was, and her life had taken a complete 180 degree turn. Where she had been focused on temporal things, she was now focused on spiritual things. Where she had been hopeless and worn out, she was now full of faith and hope and energy. When God touches a life, he wants to touch it all — every part of it. He's not interested in doing things halfway.

Because Samantha chose to follow God, the lives of hundreds of people were also changed. That day at the well, Samantha learned that you cannot ignore God, and that when you come face to face with him, in that crystal-clear pivotal moment, you must choose where you will spend eternity.

The Holy Spirit
Plugging In And Turning On

Two of the greatest events in history occurred after Jesus died: his resurrection and the coming of the Holy Spirit. Immediately after Jesus died and was buried, his disciples and followers were in shock. Scoffers taunted them: *Some messiah he turned out to be! He couldn't even save himself how could he save Israel?* And on it went. The disciples didn't understand what had happened. Yet, even though they had no idea how, they still believed that Jesus was going to make it all come out right. It wasn't long - just three days - before their faith was justified. The awesome power of God raised the physical body of Jesus from the cool slab in the garden tomb where he had been laid, caused the massive stone to be rolled away from the entrance to the tomb, and restored Jesus to life. But it was a *resurrected* life — in a glorified body — far different from the life you and I know, which is constrained by time and space and human limitations.

During those first 40 days after Jesus rose from the dead, he appeared to many people, many times, in his resurrected body. Then he made a spectacular exit from this world by ascending back to Heaven, from where he had come thirty-three years before. Just before he left them, he instructed his disciples to stay together in Jerusalem for a few days where he promised they would be filled with God's power – the Holy Spirit. Ten days later when the disciples were all together at the Jewish feast of Pentecost, God's spirit descended upon them and gave them the power they would need for the glorious, but tough, assignment he had given them: traveling to the far corners of the world to tell God's message of love and redemption through faith in Jesus Christ. There was only one reason for God to give mankind the Holy Spirit: *so they could be witnesses for him, giving evidence of everything he had said and done.* (Check out Acts 1:8)

Just so, you never need to be afraid or feel inadequate when God asks you to do a certain thing for him. His call includes the power to carry it out. If he weren't planning on doing it through you, he wouldn't have asked you to do it. And his plan doesn't include failure. All you need to do is be willing for him to use you, and stay close to him. The rest is up to him. That was true for the disciples in the first century, and it's still true in the twenty-first.

The facts of Jesus' death, resurrection, ascension, and the coming of the Holy Spirit are documented by history. If, from your perspective in the 21st century, you find it hard to believe that he really did rise from the dead, ask yourself this question: How do we know for sure that George Washington ever lived? How do we know that Moses ever lived? How do we know that man ever set foot on the moon? How do we know anything that happened before we were born? We believe these things happened because there is *evidence* that they did. There were *witnesses* who testified that a certain thing really did happen. Even after the witnesses die, we believe their testimony. We believe man walked on the moon because we believe the testimony of the men who witnessed the event, and we believe the physical evidence they submit: that first footprint in the moon dust, the moon rocks they brought back to Earth, and the American flag planted on the moon's surface, plus a whole lot more. It is neither possible nor necessary to have been there ourselves. We have faith in what the witnesses and the evidence say.

In the same way, we can't actually see the wind, but we can certainly see the evidence of it: leaves swishing in a gentle summer breeze, pristine sails billowing with wind power, eagles riding the air currents in graceful glides, giant trees snapping into pieces under the force of hurricane winds. Oh, yeah. We believe in the wind, because we can see what it does.

We can also believe in the Holy Spirit, because we can see what he does. It is possible to go through life without believing that Jesus was born, died, and rose from the dead. Each person has the power to make the decision to not believe what God has told us. But why would anyone want to? It's easier (and takes a whole lot less faith) to just believe the abundance of compelling evidence and the testimony of the witnesses who were there. The eyewitness accounts of the great events of Christianity are there for the reading — in the Bible. But in addition to that, God has given us countless pieces of evidence in the world around us. (Sunrises, for example.) If you don't believe in him, you're just not paying attention.

The Holy Spirit is not physically visible to the human eye, but the eye of faith can see what he does. The Holy Spirit is not an *it*. He is the third person of the trinity — Father, Son, and Holy Spirit – and he has a specific job to do: *The one function of the Holy Spirit is to point people to Christ.* That's it. He never calls attention to himself. It is the Holy Spirit who stirs a person's longing for God. It is the Holy Spirit who nudges us in the right direction when we don't know which way to turn. It is the Holy Spirit who empowers us to attempt great things for God. And it is the Holy Spirit who plugs us into the source of God's awesome power supply. It's not enough to be plugged in, however. You have to be *turned on!* Get excited about it! When you really know in your own spirit who God is, how much he loves you, and all the wonderful gifts he has waiting for you once you decide to give your life to him, you get turned on – big time!

As the third person of the trinity, he is as vital to an understanding of God as the Father and the Son are. He is the giver of joy and happiness. Just as it takes the shell, the white and the yolk to make a complete egg, it takes all three persons (Father, son and Holy Spirit) to make a complete Godhead. Just as no part of the egg is less important to the whole, no person of the Godhead is less important to the concept of God. It is impossible to separate the three.

Personally, I believe that every human being has three parts also: body, soul, and spirit. (That makes me a *trichotomist* in theology-speak.) The body is the physical component; the soul is the mind, emotions and will; and the spirit is the God-consciousness part. I don't believe you can separate the three and still have a whole person. When one part is sick, the whole person is affected. When all parts are healthy and functioning as God intended, the whole person is healthy and happy and productive. We are careful to feed our physical bodies, and we tend our emotions carefully, but we often neglect feeding our spirits. It is illegal in this country to fail to feed a pet, or a child, or an elderly person dependent on others for sustenance. It is just as unconscionable in God's eyes to fail to feed your spiritual nature. Not your emotions (your feel-good sensibilities) but your God-consciousness. If you have children, part of your responsibility as a parent is to teach them about God. (Just as being in a garage doesn't make a person a car, being in church doesn't automatically make a person a Christian. They don't get it by osmosis, nor do they inherit it from you. Each person has to make his or her own decision to accept God's provision for eternal security.)

It is also your responsibility to nurture your own spirit. You can start by reading and studying the Bible in order to understand God better. You can spend time talking with him in prayer. (Notice I didn't say *to* him, but *with* him. How can you hear what he has to say if you do all the talking? You have to listen, too. Prayer should be a two-way conversation.) You can attend a church where the emphasis is on the Bible. You can also surround yourself with people who believe in God.

One word of caution: you can do all these things, but still not experience the deep satisfaction of really knowing God intimately if you do not allow the Holy Spirit to teach you. Your spirit has to be willing to be taught. Here's a challenge for you: Ask him to do that. Get plugged in — to his power. And then prepare to get turned on. You'll be in for the most exciting and exhilarating time of your life! (I don't know about you, but I'm just selfish enough to want every single blessing with my name on it.)

There are four major events that are the cornerstones of the foundation of Christianity:

1. *The virgin birth of Jesus (God's incredible rescue mission to save mankind from eternal death).*
2. *The sacrificial death of Jesus (the fulfillment of God's promise to provide a way for each of us to have eternal security).*
3. *The transforming resurrection of Jesus (the sealing of our future and the source of our hope).*
4. *The coming of the Holy Spirit at Pentecost (the empowerment to carry out his wishes and change the world).*

Without any one of these, God's promises would be empty, and our faith would rest on a shaky foundation. In his infinite wisdom, God planned it all to work together for our eternal good. Is there any question in your mind that he loves you deeply?

Sapphira
All That Glitters is Not Good

After Jesus returned to Heaven and the Holy Spirit had come to indwell Christians and give them the power to carry out their commission, life became extremely busy for the disciples who had been in Jesus' inner circle of friends. What a time to be alive! This was a tremendously exciting period of history, with the disciples performing miracles one after the other and the excitement of organizing the believers into the first church. Filled with the power of God through the Holy Spirit, the disciples were whirlwinds of activity. God turned the entire world upside down with those twelve men. (Just imagine what he could do with twelve women!)

Not everyone believed the good news, however. The nature of people doesn't change much from century to century, and there were those who eagerly believed that Jesus was the Christ, but many people appeared to embrace the Gospel completely while holding back in some area of their lives. That mindset can be very hazardous to a person's health. One couple, Ananias (ANN-an-EYE-us) and Sapphira (Saff-EYE-ruh), did a perfectly human thing, and lost their lives because of it.

You've heard, no doubt, that money is the root of all evil. People often misquote that verse in I Timothy 6:10 to badmouth money. Money is not bad. That's not what Paul was saying at all. The verse actually reads, *The love of money is the root of all evil.* God knows you need money to survive in this world. That's why he invented it. The problem comes when money (and the acquiring of it) become the focus of a person's life. Money's funny that way. As soon as you get some, you want more. The more you have, the more you spend, and the more you think you need. It's an unending spiral

— not upward to a better life, but *downward* to a life that's out of balance.

In those first exciting days of the Christian church, the Apostles were busy teaching the basic principles of Christianity and showing people how to live out those principles in their everyday lives. Christianity isn't all pie in the sky by and by. It's the promise of eternal life with God, for sure, but it's also a practical formula for dealing with the daily grind. One of the outstanding characteristics of the early church was their willingness to sell everything they had and pool their resources, so that each person had enough and no one had a great excess going to waste. Believers willingly sold their land and possessions and brought the money to the Apostles to divvy up with their Christian brothers and sisters who didn't have enough to live on. It was a great concept, and it worked very well — for those whose hearts were in the right place.

One couple, however, thought they could outmaneuver God and no one would be the wiser. That little idea would be the death of them — literally. These two believers couldn't quite bring themselves to give God one hundred percent. They climbed onto the Christian bandwagon, to be sure, and sold a piece of land they had been hoarding for retirement income, and then brought the proceeds of the sale to the community pot the Apostle Peter was administering. But they didn't bring *all* the proceeds. To them, it didn't make sense to give it all away.

Can't you hear them now? *Look Sapphira, God couldn't possibly mean to give every penny away. That doesn't make sense. If we don't provide for our old age, who will? We can't trust the government to take care of us. Our kids all have families of their own and college educations to save for. We're on our own when it comes to providing a comfortable lifestyle for our old age. That's why God allowed us to make so much money: so we'd be taken care of when we're not working anymore.*

Sapphira wasn't so sure, but Ananias was her husband, after all, and he was the head of the household, so he must be right. *If you think that's what we ought to do, Honey, I'll go along with it. But we'd both better tell the same story to Peter, or we'll be in big trouble.* (She had no way of knowing just how big their trouble was going to be.)

Shrewd as always, Ananias planned every detail of how they were going to be generous with God and still provide for their

future. He laid it all out for Sapphira, and she nodded her agreement. Ananias took half of the amount they had agreed to give
God, hugged Sapphira, and left.

Arriving at the house where Peter was collecting people's
contributions, Ananias greeted the other Christians, and smiling
from ear to ear, made a big show of laying the money on top of the
pile at Peter's feet. He didn't quite look Peter in the eye, however,
and just stood there, waiting for Peter to pat him on the shoulder
and say, *Well done!* He had not counted on the Holy Spirit's telling
Peter what was really going on, however. Never one to mince words,
Peter's anger flashed out of his eyes as he looked right into the heart
and soul of Ananias and saw what he was trying to get away with.
*Ananias, why have you allowed Satan to convince you to lie to God?
While you owned the land, wasn't it yours? After you sold it, wasn't the
money all yours to do with as you chose? Why have you concocted this
stupid plan to cheat God?* Ananias was struck dumb with fear. No
defense came to his mind or his lips. He collapsed to the floor, and
died right there in front of the people he had been trying to impress
with his false generosity and good deeds. As soon as the immediate
shock wore off the crowd, several men covered him up and carried
him out and buried him. So much for the pomp and ceremony
Ananias had planned for his funeral.

Unaware of what had happened and following her husband's
instructions to the letter, three hours later, Sapphira showed up in
front of Peter with her half of the incomplete offering. With a great
display of false humility, she piously placed the moneybag on top of
the pile in front of him. She hadn't seen Ananias anywhere. Had
everything gone according to plan? Not wanting to tip her hand, she
refrained from looking around the room for her husband. As soon as
she had placed her money on the pile, Peter spoke to her. *Tell me,
Sapphira, is it true that you sold your land for this amount?* (He quoted
the price Ananias had told him.) *That's right, Peter. And here's the
other half of what we made on the sale to add to the community land.*
Peter had hoped for honesty from her.

Bitterly disappointed, he said, *Why have you agreed with your
husband to tempt the Spirit of God? Look, here come the same men who
have just buried your husband for this terrible thing you have done. Now
they will bury you, too.* Sapphira couldn't believe her ears. An icy fear

gripped her heart. How could their plan have gone so wrong? In the split second before she hit the ground, she knew the full extent of despair. The men who had carried Ananias to his grave, picked up Sapphira's lifeless body and carried her out. They buried her next to her husband, partners in crime to the end.

Right off the top of my head, I can think of about five of the Ten Commandments that Ananias and Sapphira broke, but several lessons come to mind as well. First, if there's one thing God demands from us it's honesty. It is not possible to be *half* honest and there's no such thing as a white lie. Did you ever hear the story about the two children who were playing too roughly in the family room and their mom's favorite lamp got broken? The father walks in and both kids say they didn't do it. That's about as brilliant as Ananias and Sapphira were in trying to lie to God. How futile to try to hide anything from the God who is omniscient, who made us and knows everything there is to know about us! (It gives a whole new meaning to the phrase *dumb and dumber*.)

Second, it's not smart to hold out on God. This couple had agreed to share all they had and to contribute to a common treasury to meet the common needs. They weren't forced into this agreement. It was a sacred pledge they made to God. It doesn't matter whether they weren't sincere when they made that sacred pledge, or whether they came up with the scam to impress people and cheat God after they found out how much money they had made on the sale of the property. They both wanted credit for giving everything they had. It was the same mindset that makes someone plunk a $50 bill on the top of the offering plate so everyone will see what he or she gave. That's trying to impress *people*, not God. (You *can't* impress God, so don't even try.)

Sapphira was as guilty as her husband. Wives cannot always influence husbands to do what is right, but they can try. There is no record that Sapphira even tried. She didn't have to do what she did. Each of us is responsible to God for his or her own actions. Sapphira got what she deserved. God spared not even his own son for her, and she couldn't even give him a few bucks? When you give God less than your best, what message are you giving him?

Dorcas
The Home Sewer Who Defined Joy

What gets you moving? It's been said that a person doesn't really believe a thing unless it motivates him. For example, when the alarm clock goes off some mornings, the very last thing I want to do is get out of a warm, comfortable bed. But if I don't, I'll miss a business meeting with someone who could only see me that particular day. Sometimes I don't feel like getting dinner, but if I don't, I'll snack all evening on junk food. When my brain's in gear, I know I have to crawl out of bed when the alarm goes off, and I know I have to eat a balanced, nutritious dinner. Even if I don't feel like it. If I let my feelings rule my choices, I get into trouble. Avoiding that kind of trouble keeps me motivated to do what I know I should, and avoid what I know I shouldn't. Yeah, I fall off the wagon every once in awhile, just as you do. But I'm careful to not beat myself up about it. God knows how human I am. Wonder woman, I am *not*!

In the book of Acts, chapter nine, we meet someone who was a wonder woman, if ever there was one: Dorcas. The motivating principle of this woman's life was love — love for God, which continually expressed itself in doing good for others, even those she did not know. Love got her out of bed in the morning, and kept her fingers flying all day long. Love wore out her sandals as she went from low-income housing development, to local jail, to nursing home and finally to soup kitchen. Interestingly, her name means *gazelle*. Can't you just envision her, gracefully leaping from one good deed to another, spreading joy everywhere she went? Quick and graceful, that was Dorcas.

We don't know when she first accepted Jesus as her Lord

and Savior, and we aren't told exactly how she made God the center of her life, but we do know that she loved him and embraced the Gospel with all her strength. Dorcas wasn't one to do things halfway! When she worked, she gave it everything she had, holding nothing back – living each moment to the hilt. If this woman had had a nickname, it should have been Alka-Seltzer. The gratitude and love for God just bubbled up deep inside Dorcas' spirit and effervesced all over those she came in contact with. She neither planned to be that way, nor could she help it.

It just wasn't possible to keep all that love inside, so she became a one-woman Salvation Army. Benevolent, compassionate, and generous beyond the norm, Dorcas gave so generously of her time, her talents, and her money, that 2000 years later, her name is still synonymous with gracious giving to those in need. Many churches have their *Dorcas Societies* – groups where the women do all they can to alleviate the situations of those in their communities who are in physical need. Often they collect used clothes, clean and mend them, and deliver them to those who need them. It's not unusual for a Dorcas Society to prepare entire layettes for unwed mothers of newborns one week, and knit or crochet lap robes for the local nursing home residents the next week. Because Dorcas held nothing back from God, thousands of lives have been blessed for thousands of years. We don't know if she had any children, or even if she was married. But what a legacy she left you and me!

From Dorcas we learn the formula for true joy in life. It's a simple one: God first, others next, yourself last. Some people remember the formula for *JOY* with a simple acrostic: *Jesus — Others — You.* If you keep your priorities in this order, you will be deeply, truly, unshakably, effervescently happy.

One day, Dorcas died. No warning, nothing. She just suddenly got sick and died. The women who were with her that day were in shock. *Why would God take Dorcas right in the middle of a good deed? She did so much for so many people! Didn't God know that there weren't enough people like Dorcas in the world?* The women knew that God could bring Dorcas back to life if he wanted to, just as Jesus had raised Lazarus from the dead. They sent for Peter, one of the twelve disciples who had been closest to Jesus, asking him to come immediately and bring Dorcas back to life. Peter had come a long, long way in his walk of faith. He was no longer the boisterous, impatient fisherman who galumphed through life, putting his foot in his mouth at least once a day. Peter's faith had grown incredibly strong, and he knew he didn't need to travel to Joppa to touch Dorcas in order to bring her back to life. He simply prayed – in the awesome power of the Holy Spirit, and with the unstoppable faith God had given him — that God would restore Dorcas to life. He was a simple, uneducated, rough fisherman, but God used him to do some pretty miraculous things. Back in Joppa, Dorcas opened her eyes, and picked up where she left off, never missing a stitch. Then it dawned on her what had happened. Her friends couldn't stop crying with relief and excitement. She could hardly get her breath, they were hugging her so hard! Jesus promised that those who believed in him would do miracles even greater than he had done here. This was living proof that he meant what he said.

Sometimes it is very hard to understand why people die when they do. We cannot see God's reasoning behind a young infant's crib death, a fire-fighter's life being snuffed out as he searches for people trapped in a burning apartment building, or a young teenager's losing the battle with leukemia when all of life is ahead of her. Some things we will never understand in this lifetime. We weren't meant to. I don't know the answer; I've struggled with loss myself. Through today's medical knowledge, it is not uncommon for someone whose heart has stopped beating to be brought back to life. These events are miracles, also. (God continually amazes us by insisting on working outside the box.)

If you have lost a loved one and no amount of medical expertise, and no amount of faith on your part has brought him or her back to life, you have experienced a pain like no other. All you can do when a loved one dies is hang on to God. If the grief is too much and you lose your grip, just know that God will never let go of you — even when you cannot feel his hand in yours. How do I know that? First, because I've experienced it. Second, because in Hebrews 13:5 Jesus promised, "I will never leave you nor forsake you." Whether you believe him or not doesn't change his commitment to you. If you believe that God will break his promises, then your God is too small, and that will have a big effect on how you cope with what life throws at you. You have to allow him to be God, and to work outside the box. Everything isn't black and white. Leave room in your life for unexpected miracles.

Jesus also gave us a warning, "In the world you shall have tribulation, but be of good cheer. I have overcome the world." (John 16:33) Through faith in him, you can be an overcomer, too. The Christian life was never designed to be a walk on the beach on a sunny day. Some days it's downright tough, and simply too much. Those are the days when the Dorcas formula will work for you: *Jesus Others, and You.* When you are overwhelmed with grief, or circumstances keep knocking you down, step outside your own box and do something for someone who needs a little help or encouragement. It's the best antidote for grief that I know, and the best formula for true JOY!

Lydia

The Businesswoman Who Made God Her C.E.O.

Lydia was a successful and influential businesswoman who lived in the bustling city of Philippi, in Macedonia, a country between the Adriatic and Aegean Seas, now Europe. She was a seller of purple, literally a trader of purple cloth. That doesn't sound like much of a claim to fame today, but in the days before polyester and synthetic dyes, the color purple was reserved for those who could afford it. Her clientele probably included the Roman imperial family, who wore the royal purple on state occasions. The purple dye itself was made from the secretions of a certain shellfish (mussels), and the juice turned purple only when exposed to the sun's rays.

Lydia made her living by dyeing. Producing the dye, and dyeing the fabric required knowledge and skill. This career gal had both. The Bible doesn't state whether Lydia was single or not. My vote is that she was, because she devoted so much time and effort to her business, as her prosperity proved. Single or not, Lydia was on a career path to the top of her profession. She probably was a member of the Dyer's Guild, a prototype chamber of commerce. Today if we want a couple of yards of purple silk or wool, we drive the car to the local fabric store and choose from at least a dozen shades and weights. Not in Lydia's day. It took guts for a woman to be successful in business in the 1st century. (Two thousand years later, not much has changed, has it?) Lydia had all the right stuff: determination, foresight, solid work ethic, opportunity, and a small market niche that could afford her product.

There was something else Lydia had, however, that no amount of money could take care of: a God-shaped space in her life that nothing else could fill. For all her success in business, something

122

was missing. She discovered what it was one day when two missionaries, Paul and Silas, showed up in her city.

The Bible says that Lydia worshipped God. We are not told how it happened that she had a knowledge of Israel's God, but however she learned about him, she loved him and believed in him. At the point where we meet her in Acts 16:14, she had not yet heard that the Messiah had come, that his name was Jesus, and that he had provided the solution to every problem any human being could ever have. Lydia was so ready to receive that message! God had prepared her spirit to respond to the Gospel, and she hung on Paul's every word as he spoke to the small group of people she had assembled to hear him. Businesswoman that she was, as soon as Paul finished speaking, she acted decisively. She asked to be baptized as a symbol of her faith in Christ, and those who were part of her household were baptized at the same time. Then she gave the two missionaries a warm, gracious invitation to stay at her home that they could not refuse.

Those must have been glorious days for Lydia and her fellow believers. No matter how much Paul and Silas taught them about their new Christian life, they couldn't get enough. They were like sponges, soaking up everything they could learn about Jesus and what he had done for them. Unlike sponges, however, they didn't just keep all the blessings to themselves. They spread the word from Philippi to neighboring towns. Lydia told her customers. New Christians were added to the Philippi church every week. From that one small beginning in the home of a businesswoman who was 100% sold out to God, an entire world was reached with the life-changing Gospel of Jesus Christ. The world would never be the same again.

At some time in every person's life, he or she is faced with a pivotal decision: *What do I do with Jesus? Do I ignore him? Do I reject him? Or do I accept him with joy and gratitude?* When you realize who Jesus is and invite him to become Lord of your life, he doesn't come in on the installment plan. When God enters your life, he holds nothing back: you get all of him. (Even if you don't use it all or understand it all, it's all available to you, bought and paid for with Christ's sacrificial death for you. Think of it as a shelf in Heaven with a lot of presents – love, joy, peace, hope, faith, strength, wisdom — all wrapped beautifully and every one of them has *your* name on it. It's up to you to claim them and make them your own.) Because God gives 100% for us, he expects 100% in return. There's no such thing as being a partial Christian. Either you are, or you aren't. If you were born into the Smith family, for example, are you a Smith one day, and the next day a Johnson? Even if you marry, or change your name legally, you will always be a Smith, born into the Smith family with all its quirks and foibles, all its privileges and responsibilities. Try as you might to divorce yourself from the Smiths, deep down you will always be one. Just so, when you are born into Christ's family, you take his name (*Christ*- ian), and from that moment on, you belong to him. You'll never have to wonder who you are, or where you fit in, not ever again. Becoming a member of God's family is the 100% solution to everything. Just as being a Christian involves a 100% of your life. You cannot be a Christian just on Sunday mornings from 10 a.m. to 11 a.m. God is 100% committed to you; you need to be 100% committed to him — in every area of your life.

For the rest of her life, Lydia's house remained a haven to Christians, a place where they could be refreshed in body and spirit. She helped organize the local church in Philippi, the same local group to whom Paul wrote the book of Philippians. This woman knew a business secret that is not included in the course of study for any M.B.A. or business degree. This one concept is both effective and efficient in turning a business around. This one idea alone can make a tremendous difference in a business' bottom line.

Want to know the secret? She made God her C.E.O. — and he made her business flourish. (Duh. Can it really be that simple? I've been in business since 1985 and I'm here to tell you it *is*.) In Philippians 4:19, Paul told Lydia's little band of believers, "...God shall supply all your need, according to his riches in glory, by Christ Jesus." If you think Christianity and business don't mix, there's nothing wrong with Christianity. There's something wrong with your business.

Phebe
The Loyal Rural Mail Carrier

I remember when a first-class postage stamp cost ten cents. (Now I've dated myself, haven't I!) Yet, even though the cost of communicating has steadily risen over the past twenty years, it's still very cost-effective to send a letter. Just imagine what it was like for the Apostle Paul to try to communicate with the fledgling churches springing up like wildfire all over the known world. E-mail hadn't yet been invented, and snail-mail doesn't even begin to describe it! The Roman government had mail carrier service, but it was not for the use of the public. All the Apostles faced a daunting task that would have stopped lesser men cold: how to facilitate the encouragement and teaching of these new churches that were multiplying faster than the proverbial rabbits. They were all full of excitement and enthusiasm (and problems), and needed guidance and a good solid foundation of sound doctrine if they were to endure. Most of the New Testament is the result of this need to instruct and ground these baby churches. (It's amazing to me that the instruction and advice written two thousand years ago is every bit as relevant in today's churches. Basic human nature hasn't changed.) The Apostles wrote their hearts out, pouring out their love and instruction in long, laboriously crafted epistles. (There were no pads of paper and no felt-tip pens, either.) Still, the writing was the easy part.

The hard part was delivering the letters to their destinations. Remember now, that the only means of transportation was either by ship or overland by caravan. The best and most trustworthy method was to have each letter hand-carried by a trusted messenger. To deliver his letter to the church at Rome (the book of Romans in the Bible), Paul chose Phebe (FEE-bee), a leader in a little church near the city of Corinth. She was a trusted friend of the Apostle Paul.

Phebe was very pleased to have been chosen for the job. She carefully mapped out her trip, determining the safest and best route to follow. It would not be an easy trip, by any stretch of the imagination, but it would be richly rewarding to Phebe, both personally and spiritually.

Being a rural mail earner did have its drawbacks, however. Since lengthy travel for an unescorted woman was slightly danger-ous in those days, she probably joined a caravan for as long as she could, and then crossed by boat into Roman territory, finally making her way to Rome. Along the way she stopped at as many Christian churches as possible, to bring them greetings from Paul, and other Christians as well. The people at the little churches were always glad to meet believers from other cities, and everyone wanted to talk long into the night. Jet-lagged, travel-fatigued, saddle-sore from all the horseback riding, missing her own little comfortable bed back home, and sick to death of fried chicken and mashed potatoes (*Didn't these people know how to cook anything else???*), Phebe exer-cised extreme grace under pressure. And then the next day, she got up to do it all again, reciting her mantra: *Neither snow, nor rain, nor dark of night shall keep this courier from her appointed rounds.*[2] She had made a commitment to God when she had given her heart to him, and she had made a promise to Paul to deliver this letter. He had trusted and honored her by asking her to deliver the letter. Nothing was going to keep her from doing that. *Nothing!*

Phebe's strengths were her utter trustworthiness and loyalty. Her motivation was love. Her creed was service — to God and to his people. She kept her promise to Paul, and delivered the letter to the group of believers at Rome. We know from other portions of Scripture that Phebe was respected and loved by all who worked in the church with her, and that she gave of herself unreservedly, no matter what she was doing. Everything this woman did was done in service to God. If she had a grave marker, it would have read: *She gave her very best back to God.*

[2] *Inscription on the General Post Office, New York City, 8th Avenue and 33rd Street. This inscription was supplied by William Mitchell Kendall of the architectural firm of McKim, Mead & White, who designed the New York General Post Office.*

Eunice and Lois
Using Their Influence

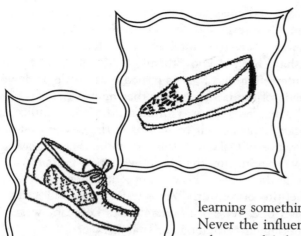

My father used to say, "You can learn something from everyone, even if it's to not be like him." I have never heard a truer statement. The flip side is that someone is learning something from you. Never the influence you have in other people's lives. Case in point: two women named Eunice and Lois. Lois was the older of the two. Her daughter, Eunice, was the mother of Timothy, a thoroughly wonderful young man who threw himself without reservation into Christian service at age 15 when he heard the Apostle Paul preach.

Timothy loved his grandmother and mother, of course. Their sincere love for God was evident to anyone who met them. If the eyes are the window of the soul, these two women must have had the most gorgeous eyes in the country, for out of them shone hope, joy, peace and a deep beauty of spirit. Paul used the word *unfeigned* to describe the essence of their faith, meaning without hypocrisy.

These two women had that rare quality about them that made everyone feel better for having been in their presence. It would be wrong to assume they were perfect, because they weren't. And they freely admitted it. Who wouldn't get frustrated when her darling baby boy filled three diapers one right after the other? Who wouldn't be upset when chubby little fingers found their way into the flour bin and dusted the new couch with the fluffy white stuff? Who wouldn't lose her patience with a toddler's unceasing repetition of the word *Why?* Lois and Eunice were, after all, only human. But they were able to laugh at themselves when they made a mistake, and cheerfully refused to take themselves (or Timmy's baby antics) too seriously. The quality that made these two so special, however, was their total lack of pretense. How refreshing it must have been to know them!

It was an interesting set of genes passed on to little Timmy. No mention is made of the father, except that he was a Greek. He probably died when Timothy was an infant. Lois and Eunice were not Greek, but Jewish. Their home was in the city of Lystra, in the Roman province of Galatia. For the grandmother to play such a conspicuous role in Timothy's life, the mother must have had to work outside the home. The word grandmother appears only once in the entire Bible: in the Apostle Paul's second letter to Timothy, chapter one, verse 5, in reference to Lois. She was integral to his upbringing and character-shaping years.

Paul loved Timothy as a son from the moment they met, when he responded to the tug of the Holy Spirit on his heart, and gave his life to Christ to do with as he saw fit — what we refer to as *conversion*, or *being born again*. From that moment, Timothy's life took a major turn. He had always loved God and followed the faith of his mother and grandmother. But it had never been so intensely personal before. Never one to do things halfway, Timothy tagged along with Paul every chance he got. A wonderful friendship grew between the two, and when Paul set out after a second visit to Lystra, Timothy left with him.

Timothy was Paul's constant companion, fellow missionary, substitute son, and closest confidante for many more years than any other person. When he was imprisoned for his faith, it was to Timothy that Paul turned for comfort and support. And he was not disappointed. Because of that young man's upbringing, because of the influence of both his grandmother and his mother, Paul was able to entrust him with the most delicate missions and to put him in charge of the most important congregations. Timothy grew into a man of generosity, unselfishness, deep devotion to God, and a wonderful charm and gentleness that endeared him to all who knew him. Everyone should have a son like that! What a blessing he was to everyone — all because he had a godly mother and grandmother who taught him well.

The lesson for us is plain. *Live your life as if a child were watching, because one probably is.* If you have no young, impressionable children in your life, you undoubtedly know people younger than you (if not in years, then in their Christian lives). They, too, are watching you, learning from your example. Make sure it's a good one.

Priscilla
Sharing The Fruit Of Her Loom

Have you ever studied a piece of fabric? I mean really studied it? I am not a weaver, but I am fascinated with the result of taking two threads and weaving them together — back and forth, up and down, over and under, warp and woof – until you have a strong, solid piece of cloth that is both useful and decorative. A good relationship is like that. (And I *don't* mean one is warped and the other one barks!) Each partner contributes his or her strengths that equalize the other's weaknesses. Together they are stronger than they could be alone. The result is a strong unit that can withstand whatever life brings.

Last week, I performed a wedding ceremony on a pontoon boat anchored in a quiet cove on the lake where I live. It was the most fun (and the most touching) wedding I have ever attended. The couple asked me to read the following verses from the thirteenth chapter of First Corinthians, from the Living Bible:

Love is very patient and kind, never jealous or envious, never boastful or proud, never haughty or selfish or rude. Love does not demand its own way. It is not irritable or touchy. It does not hold grudges and will hardly even notice when others do it wrong. It is never glad about injustice, but rejoices whenever truth wins out. If you love someone, you will be loyal to him no matter what the cost. You will always believe in him, always expect the best of him, and always stand your ground in defending him.

That says it all, I think. Love covers a multitude of sins. Priscilla and Aquila (ah-KWIIL-lah), a first-century wife and ecclesiastical limb here, but that's what the Bible and history both say.)

130

It's only *people* who get hung up on gender issues. We learn from the Bible that there is no gender gap in Heaven, because there is no gender. God gives his individual children different gifts and talents so they can use them to help others, and he does not differentiate between women's talents and men's talents. It takes all of us working together, using all our combined talents, to fulfill the commission God gave us when Jesus returned to Heaven: "Go ye into all the world and preach the Gospel...." (Mark 16:15)

If God gives you a gift, you can be sure he intends you to use it. Priscilla used her gift for teaching and expounding Scripture to nurture a multitude of young Christians and grow them into strong examples of vibrant faith who, in turn, taught other young Christians. Those Christians then taught others. And so it went, generation after generation, century after century, until here we sit, you and I.

I have learned much over the years; therefore, much is required of me. If I do not use my God-given gifts of teaching and writing to share what I have learned, I will have to answer for that someday. Just so, if you do not use what I have shared with you to help others, you will have to answer for that someday as well. None of us lives unto ourselves. We *need* each other. For that reason, and because this has been all one-sided so far I'd be delighted if you'd share with me something God has taught you. Who knows? Maybe it will be enough for a second book!

An Invitation

You may think you are just an ordinary person, with no particular claim to fame, and you may think God could never use you to change anyone's life, much less change the world. The fact is, if you are living your life for God, you may never know in this lifetime how God has used you to bless others. The simple truth is that God doesn't always use the wise people of the world, the wealthy, or those in positions of authority to spread his love to the world. He doesn't need our abilities, you see. He just needs our *availability*. All God wants from each of us is our willingness to be a simple conduit through which he can flow.

Are you willing for God to use you? Are you willing to let his love, his blessings, his wisdom to flow through you to change the lives of those he brings across your path? If your answer is *yes*, turn the page....

Dear   Reader,

It is my personal belief that God cares very deeply about each and every one of us, and that is what I've tried to illustrate in this book. I also believe that the most important thing a woman can do for herself, for her husband, her children and her world is cultivate a personal relationship with God. It's worked for me for 39 years now, and I know it will make a difference in your life, too.

God is looking for women to bless the world. Would you like to be one of them? If you would like to offer your life to God for him to use as he has used the women in these stories, it's very simple to do. Just tell him you want him to take your life (warts and all) and use it to bless others. Then thank him for doing what you've asked. And then hang on with anticipation, *expecting* him to bless you, and others as well.

You might like to cement this decision in your mind by signing and dating this page on the lines below, and keep it in your Bible or daily journal.

N a m e   D a t e

_____   _____

There's so much more to God than any one of us can imagine! If you are interested in knowing more about him and the Bible, I would be happy to send you a helpful and informative booklet.. No strings attached - except the heartstrings, of course. Send your request via E-mail to Alice@YourAuthor.com

God   Bless!

Alice Anderson Alice   Anderson

ORDER FORM

To order additional copies of *Through The Bible In High Heels*, please use the order form below.

Ordered by: (please print)

Name _____

Address _____

City _____ State/Prov._____

Postal/Zip Code _____ Tel. _____

Ship to: (if different address from above)

Name _____

Address _____

City _____ State/Prov._____

Postal/Zip Code _____ Tel. _____

Copies@ 14.95 (U.S. funds)	$ _____	
Shipping ($2.00 first book – $.50 each add. book)	$ _____	
Total (U.S. Funds)	$ _____	

Payment Method:

☐ Check ☐ Money Order

Make Check/Money Order payable to and mail to:
Power Publications, Inc.
573 Fox Hunt Circle
Longwood FL 32750

*To order by phone and pay by credit card
call Essence Publishing at 1-800-238-6376
and have your credit card handy.*

Quantity discounts available. Call (407) 321-6137 for rates.